New Earth Fast

Cleanse to Enlighten Yourself

TONI TONEY

Copyright 2025
Toni Toney: All rights reserved

This book may not be reproduced in whole or in part without written permission from Toni Toney except by a reviewer who may quote brief passages; nor may any part of this book be reproduced, republished, stored in a retrieval system, or transmitted in any form or by any means, electronic, mechanical, photocopying, recording, or other by any individual, organization or corporation without written permission from Toni Toney and New Earth Publishers.

DISCLAIMER: The nutritional and health information provided in this book is intended for educational purposes only. All efforts have been made to ensure the accuracy of the information contained in this book as of the date published. Nothing listed or mentioned in this book should be considered as medical advice or a substitute for medical advice for dealing with stress or any other medical problem. Consult your health-care professional for individual guidance on specific health issues and before following this or any program. Persons with serious medical conditions should seek professional care. The author and publisher specifically disclaim any liability, loss or risk, personal or otherwise, which is incurred as a consequence, directly or indirectly, of the use and application of the contents of this book.

Printed in the United States of America.

Book cover and layout design by keenankreative.com

First Edition
Published by: New Earth Publishers 2025

CONTENTS

PRAISES FOR TONI'S TEACHINGS IV

THE SUN AND THE MOON V

1 | THE GREAT AWAKENING 1
   Prophetic Awakenings

2 | SHIFT WITH THE NEW MOON 31
   Blood–Our Inner Red Sea

3 | THE POWER OF THE NEW MOON FAST 45
   Our Body's Internal Waterways

4 | THE ANCIENT ART OF FASTING,
   FORGIVENESS, AND PRAYER 69
   Cleanse Out the Old and Shift Into the New

5 | THE NEW EARTH FAST 113
   Cleanse to Enlighten Yourself

6 | WHAT TO EAT AFTER THE FAST 163
   Eat to Enlighten Yourself

PRAISES FOR TONI'S TEACHINGS

"This book is powerful! The knowledge of fasting during the 7-day new moon phase is both unique and needed in today's toxic world. Bless you, Toni Toney, for bringing back the lost knowledge of Luna, the moon of planet Earth, in this most amazing book!"

–Don Tolman, the Real Food Medicine Man

This book is a thoughtful, scientifically researched, journey to improve one's mind, body and spiritual health. It touches on cutting edge science of brain immunology with mindfulness and dietary techniques. There is positiveness in each page to enrich all aspects of the soul. This insightful journey with Toni Toney teaches how to change one's life.

–Dr. Lorne Label, Neurologist

"Toni's knowledge on health and the body is invaluable. I am forever grateful for meeting her and learning the ways for a healthier life in every way!"

–Jenna Tatum, America Actress, Former Model, and Dancer

THE SUN AND THE MOON

The sun and the moon are two great lights. They dance amongst the stars in the heavens, affecting us in ways mostly unknown to the conscious mind. They serve as signs to mark the seasons of change; the light and the dark, the dawn and the dusk, the sunrise and the sunset—the letting go of the old and the shifting into the new.

Throughout time, the relationship between these two great lights has been dynamic, ever evolving the patterns of life on Earth and the great cycles of change. The only dynamic that has changed is our relationship with them. But we must now pay attention, for they serve as signs for the end of an age. Follow their rhythms and watch as the world within and around you shift.

The time has come. The veil between heaven and earth is lifting. The sun is shining its illuminating rays upon the darkness of the world. All that is evil is being exposed. We must prepare ourselves.

The *New Earth Fast* is how!

VI NEW EARTH FAST

– 1 –
THE GREAT AWAKENING
Prophetic Awakenings

There's a growing sense of unease in the air—an unsettling uncertainty about the future, as if a major shift is unfolding. People around the world are consumed by apocalyptic rumors, each culture grappling with its own version of what's to come. Some call it the "Great Awakening," others the "end of the world," but one thing is clear: something transformative is happening.

I began writing this book in 1979—though, more accurately, it began writing me. Though I wasn't physically holding pen and paper, the words were already written on my heart, waiting to be shared. Back then, I often wondered, "Why me?" when a Angelic Presence appeared and began delivering prophecic awakenings of a world-altering shift—a shift that is unfolding now.

My Awakening
Raised in a small-town patriarchal tradition, I struggled with the idea of a judgmental God, especially as a woman. From birth, I was taught that women were temptresses—blamed for the fall of humanity as descendants of Eve. Every sermon felt like a tightening noose around my neck, choking off the power of my feminine existence, and the

idea of Judgment Day left me questioning how a loving God could condemn us.

By the age of 16, I rejected the church and its teachings. But by the time I was 30, everything shifted. I began experiencing a deep, personal relationship with God that shattered my old beliefs. This was the beginning of my Great Awakening—a shift from "The Fall" into what I now call "The Return."

This book is a prophetic guide—a journey that shows us how to prepare our physical bodies for what I call the shift of the ages—a shift from a "fallen state of physical consciousness" to an "ascended state of spiritual consciousness." And when we wake up and our spiritual eyes are open, we will once again remember who we truly are and what we are capable of.

This is the Great Awakening.

PROPHETIC AWAKENING #1
An Angelic Presence Appears

I awoke, startled, in the middle of the night. Hovering above me was an Angelic Presence crowned with a golden halo of shimmering light. The brilliance radiating from this golden being was beyond anything I had ever seen or felt before. It was as though I was being lifted into a higher dimension.

Words of prophecy were spoken…

You are frightened. Have no fear. For what I have come to tell you is already known by you and all who have been given this precious breath of life.

The breath that breathes your physical body—it's a miracle. You have simply taken it for granted because you fail to remember who and what you truly are.

And if you fail to purify yourself and pierce through your physical body's thick, dense veil of illusion, you will surely die.

So, prepare yourself, for the end is coming soon.

But remember this—there is no end to this end—it is simply the beginning of that which never ends. For each end you reach is but a little death which are steppingstones to the ultimate death of who and what you think you are.

And as you walk this narrow, arduous path, you will feed on hidden manna and be given a new name. Behold! The book of Seven Seals is about to be opened! But the greatest mystery of all is this...

Your physical body is the book of Seven Seals to be opened in the last days.

I watched in awe as the Angelic Presence took a slow inhalation, then dissolved itself back into the dark of the night.

I was bewildered, unable to make sense of it all.

Weeks later, still consumed by the mystery of that moment, I woke in a feverish sweat. I couldn't walk and was rushed to the hospital. After a series of examinations and blood tests, the doctors admitted me to isolation due to a dangerously low white blood cell count. Despite rounds of the strongest intravenous antibiotics, my white blood cell count continued to plummet.

Even the most renowned immunologists studying my case were stumped. They blamed my declining count on some mysterious, antibiotic-resistant bug. But they couldn't explain it, nor could they find a cure.

A few days later, my family was called in. We received the worst news ever: I was at a tipping point. If my white blood cell count didn't rise by morning, I wouldn't make it. Tears streamed down my face at the thought of leaving my two young children, who peered through the isolation room window. My son was six, my daughter only four. They were far too young to lose their mother.

In that moment, I began pleading with God for help. I had to live—if not for me, for them.

As the stillness of the night enveloped me, I closed my eyes. A deep sense of calm washed over me, and I became acutely aware of the subtle breeze of my breath moving in and out of my nostrils.

Then, once again, the Angelic Presence appeared above me. We began communicating telepathically, our connection more felt than spoken, like a profound exchange that bypassed words.

I said, *I'm dying, and they have no cure for me.*

The Angelic Presence replied, *how can they possibly have a cure when they don't understand your real problem?*

I asked, *so what's my real problem?*

The Angelic Presence said, *the illusion that you're separate from God, from nature, and from everything and everyone around you.*

If you will but focus upon your breath—the Breath of God who breathed your soul into physical existence—you will live!

A deafening silence filled the room. I watched in awe as the Angelic Presence began to breathe—in and out, in and out—dissolving with each inhalation, then returning to visible form with each exhalation.

Entranced by the sight, I synchronized my breath with the rhythm of the Angelic Presence above me.

With each inhale and exhale, I felt my body shift from its dense, physical form into something lighter, less tangible.

As I continued the rhythm for what felt like hours, a deep, visceral understanding settled within me: not only was it the Breath of God breathing me, but I knew—without a doubt—that I was, in essence, more SPIRIT than PHYSICAL.

Through the power of my breath, the physical "coat of skin" that had once veiled my Spirit grew thin, as though I were being shown how to return to my original, Edenic state of being. What a mind-altering, soul-shifting reality that was!

Moments later, the Angelic Presence took one final, long inhalation—and then... *poof,* it was gone.

I fell into a deep, profound sleep.

The next morning, I awoke with the undeniable sense that a part of me had died that night, and a new me had been born. The world I had once known was slipping away.

After a series of blood tests, my primary physician entered my room, his face a mix of confusion and disbelief.

He said...

> *"I have no idea what happened during the night, but your white blood cell count is normal. It's a miracle!"*

Ecstatic, my family rushed into my once isolation room. There wasn't a dry eye. But deep inside, I knew that what seemed like the end of a miraculous story was, in truth, only the first steppingstone on a journey to discover who and what I truly am.

Every joint and muscle in my body ached, as though I were preparing to confront yet another false belief about myself.

PROPHETIC AWAKENING #2
Live Where the Change Is

That night, before falling asleep, I closed my eyes and breathed the breath of God into my pain-ridden body. The deeper my in-and-out breath dropped into the sensation of the pain, the less intense it became. Though I couldn't visually see the Angelic Presence above me, I could feel its subtle essence surrounding me.

With my eyes closed, I heard…

> *Love the pain; don't resist its strain.*
>
> *When you live life through old memories, you turn to stone. And live life not for tomorrow, for each day holds its own.*
>
> *To live each moment in the who you are makes for brighter tomorrows. For you are the seconds, the minutes, the hours of time. Time is but an illusion, so set it free.*
>
> *When there is pain in your life and things seem uncertain, you must go within yourself so I can lift the veil of mortality's curtain.*
>
> *Learn to live where the change is, for you are one with nature, which is constantly evolving.*
>
> *You are one with the earthquake that opens from great shifts and change. You are one with the tornado with whirling thoughts*

of confusion. You are one with the volcano whose fiery emotions build then erupt. You are one with the stormy seas, so learn to ride them, then feel the calm.

You are one with nature, which is constantly changing.

Do you truly want to become one with "the light of the world?"

I nodded my head and replied, *I do!*

Then come through your darkness, for fear is your darkness and love is your light.

So, learn to love where the change is, for LOVE is who you truly are!

With that profound awakening, I fell into a deep, almost hypnotic sleep.

When I woke the next morning, although the pain wasn't completely gone, it had subsided. As my consciousness shifted, I continued to consider the idea of my oneness with nature.

As fate would have it, standing in the doorway of my once isolated room was a longtime friend. After I shared with him what had happened to me that night, he began sharing his own story—how he, too, had faced death and experienced what others called a miracle.

It was his return to nature and eating foods grown by nature that healed him. He had stopped consuming an unnatural diet high in processed foods, meat, and dairy, and shifted to a natural diet rich in organic regenerative plant foods.

He spoke about how Hippocrates (460-370 BC), the father of medicine, healed the sick by using food as medicine instead of drugs, along with other practices such as fasting, detoxifying herbs, regenerative plant foods, spring water, hot and cold baths, and plenty of sunlight. After following Hippocrates' healing regimen for several months, he experienced his own miracle!

As he was leaving, he glanced at my IV bag filled with drugs dripping into my veins and firmly said...

"Nature heals, not drugs!"

He then suggested that I check myself out of man's hospital and into nature's hospital so nature could heal me from the inside out.

And so, I did. Three months later, I had experienced nature's miracle. The excruciating pain in my joints and muscles was completely gone. I had followed my friend's Hippocratic advice—juicing, blending, fasting, eating, and cleansing my way back to wellness!

With that, my family and I decided it would be more conducive to my new lifestyle to live in a warmer climate, rather than the freezing winter of Chicago. So, we packed everything up and moved to the tropical Gulf Coast of southern Florida—a climate offering year-round sunshine, fruit trees, and vegetable gardens.

It was heavenly!

PROPHETIC AWAKENING #3
The Table

A few months later, another prophetic awakening occurred. One warm, breezy night, as I walked along the crystalline, white sands of the coast under the full moon, I heard a still, small voice within me whisper…

Though the road that you travel may seem to bend and turn,
Know my saints are there with you, these bends are so you'll learn.

The world as you have known, it is passing away.
In its destruction, know I am there with you each and every day.

As your mission unfolds in the midst of war…
Look not to the left, nor to the right, but keep your eyes on my face and see what it's there for.

For these wars and these rumors of war, they are within each of us. Fill your heart with LOVE, and watch—ashes to ashes, dust to dust.

For the old is now passing with each breath that you take.
The New Earth is emerging; this world must shake.

Teaching Divine Love through the foods that you eat,
Bringing people into your home and washing their feet.

For this bread, it is my body; take, eat, and remember Me.
This drink, it is my blood; drink it with love.

This table has been set for all those who see.
Your house will be filled.

The people, they are longing to be set free—
Set free from the belief that they are separate from Me.
             -Christ

I was speechless. As I drove home, I reflected on the idea that the foods we eat could be a type of communion. Most religious circles partake in communion on the Sabbath—usually through a wafer and wine, symbols of the body (wafer) and blood (wine) of Christ. But it felt as though I was awakening to a deeper, hidden understanding of Christ and communion, one that extended far beyond what many of us have been taught.

The questions that kept swirling in my mind were...

- Is it possible that Christ—the light of the world—is calling us to sit at the table together in a consciousness of communion as we partake of an array of colorful plant foods—foods created by the light of the sun, also deemed as—the light of the world? When we do, are we partaking of the body of the plant and drinking its blood?
- Is it possible that our physical bodies are truly a temple, and that food is an offering to Christ who dwells within us?
- Is it possible that Christ—the light of the world—through the power of photosynthesis, gifts us with an abundance of vibrant plant foods to fill our physical bodies with light? After all, photosynthesis comes from two words: *photo*, means "light," and *synthesis*, means "to make."

- Is it possible that by consuming an array of colorful plant foods, we are literally "eating light," transforming our physical bodies into a "body of light?"

After days of deep reflection, I discovered that the primary molecule of hemoglobin in human blood mirrors the molecule of chlorophyll in plant blood—except for one key difference: the central element of iron in hemoglobin is replaced by magnesium in chlorophyll. While iron in our blood is essential for oxygen transport, magnesium gives chlorophyll the ability to absorb sunlight and convert it into the energy of life.

In essence, when we partake of an array of colorful plant foods—whether eating the whole plant (bread) or drinking its juice (blood)—through the power of photosynthesis, we are literally eating and drinking the body and blood of Christ—the light of the world—so that our physical bodies can shift into a "body of light!"

I was awestruck by yet another insight.

- Is it possible that this is the true purpose and power of food? That our diets are not about counting fats, calories, carbohydrates, or protein?

This was a challenging revelation, but it struck me deeply. Then, I discovered that the spiritual meaning of "bread" is *divine substance*, also known as hidden manna, which refers to partaking in the very substance of Christ. This *divine substance* is everywhere, ever-present, and exists within everyone. The key is learning how to partake of it, how to truly "eat of it."

"I have food to eat that ye know not of."
—John 4:32

PROPHETIC AWAKENING #4
The Shift of the Ages

Soon after this prophetic awakening, I began teaching classes based on the concept of "food as communion." One such seminar took me to Malibu, California, where I arrived just days after a major 6.8 earthquake. Although I was a bit hesitant due to the possibility of aftershocks, deep down, I knew I was meant to be there.

After the class, an elderly gentleman invited me to break bread with him at a local organic, plant-based restaurant. As we ate lunch, another major earthquake rolled through the café floor like a massive ocean wave. Without thinking, I dove under the table as everything around us began to fall. My new friend followed suit. It was the scariest thing I had ever experienced. My entire body shook, as if in sync with the earthquake itself.

Later that night, as I was trying to fall asleep, the Angelic Presence appeared above me once again, bringing with it another, almost demanding, prophetic awakening.

The Angelic Presence declared...

> *Your mission is to help people get their physical bodies ready; there's a change coming!*

Still trembling, I asked, *what?*

The Angelic Presence repeated, *your mission is to help people get their physical bodies ready; there's a change coming! And when the physical body is ready...*

It's in the breath!

I watched as the Angelic Presence took a slow inhalation and completely dissolved into the air. Then it took a slow exhalation and reappeared in visible form, saying...

It's in the breath!

Then, poof! The Angelic Presence was gone.

Confused and unsure how to proceed, I closed my eyes and meditated in total silence, seeking understanding about this new mission I had been given. My mind kept asking the same question over and over..;.

So, what is the greatest thing we can do to prepare our physical bodies for this change that's coming?

Then suddenly, the Angelic Presence appeared once again, answering...

You must understand that your immune system is the key to the answer you seek! It is in synch with the planet's moon cycles.

Im-mune means I'm-moon.

For 21 days, your immune system waxes (increases), and for 7 days, it wanes (decreases).

Like your planet, your physical body is made up mostly of water. Water ebbs and flows according to the waxing and waning of the moon—so too does your immune system.

During the 7-day waning phase of the new moon, the viscosity of the blood thins, greatly aiding the physical body in cleansing out the old and shifting into the new.

Fasting on an array of colorful plant foods, along with forgiveness and prayer during the 7-day new moon phase, is the greatest thing you can do to prepare your physical body for the shift of the ages.

The time has come to go to the island of Patmos, where you will be given seven keys to prepare you for the shift of the ages—the shift from the fallen state of physical consciousness into the ascended state of spiritual consciousness.

I couldn't pack my bags fast enough. As fate would have it, my plane landed on the island of Kos in Greece, where Hippocrates, the father of medicine, once taught his students the healing power of plant foods. From there, I would travel the next day by boat to the island of Patmos.

After checking into my hotel, I made my way to the ancient ruins where the Hippocratic Hospital once stood. It was there that I met a Hippocratic botanist working in the gardens surrounding the hospital's museum. He graciously walked me through the winding rows of fruit trees and berry bushes, teaching me that plant foods were not only 'medicine' for the body, but also for the mind and spirit.

What fascinated me most was when he shared how Hippocrates discovered that nature produced what he called "plant inoculators," which were abundantly found in berries. He explained that by eating lots of berries, our bodies will create a powerful immunity to almost everything.

From a spiritual perspective, Hippocrates also believed that berries, because they create inner strength and resilience, also form an outer protective shield around the body, protecting us from external pathological, emotional, and mental influences. In essence, no matter what is happening in the world, we are divinely protected.

Needless to say, the grounds were covered with berry bushes!

That evening, after breaking bread with the botanist, I excused myself and walked down to the seashore. I sat on the sandy beach, gazing out upon the blue waters of the Aegean Sea. The night was alive with the magic of a full moon… my eyes danced with the shimmering beams of light on the moonlit waters.

Enchanted by the spirit of my surroundings, I reflected on the synchronistic way I had met the Hippocratic botanist and how the Angelic Presence had said that our immune system is key to preparing our physical bodies for the shift of the ages. I was ready. So, I made my way to the town square in search of berries!

PROPHETIC AWAKENING #5
The Book of Seven Seals

That night, sleep eluded me. My mind was consumed with the thought that my physical body is the Book of Seven Seals—waiting to be opened in the last days. As dawn approached, I hurriedly made my way to the 5 AM ferry bound for the island of Patmos. It was here, in the Cave of the Apocalypse, where Saint John received his visions of the end times, as recorded in the Book of Revelation. My prayer, heartfelt and urgent, was that I might gain an even deeper understanding of how to open our physical body's book of seven seals.

Once the ferry docked, I checked into my hotel, caught a taxi, and made my way to the cave. The moment I walked in, history seemed to linger in the air. The stillness was palpable, as if the walls were echoing with the prayers and visions Saint John had once experienced here. The crack in the ceiling, above the spot where he had knelt to receive divine revelations, remained visible—a silent testament to the mysteries held within these walls.

The only other person in the cave was a monk, his presence serene and undisturbed by the sacred atmosphere. His meditative silence seemed to bring with it unspoken revelations, grounding me amidst my swirling thoughts. My mind raced with questions, doubts, and a desperate yearning for understanding.

The seven seals of the body—what did they represent? How could one begin to open them?

The monk sat down next to me; it was the same spot where St. John received the Book of Revelation. His eyes closed, his breath steady, as though he had already discovered the answers I sought. His stillness felt like an anchor, offering a quiet strength that seemed to transcend words. I closed my eyes, preparing myself for what was about to unfold. I focused on the deep stillness of the cave, letting the cool, ancient air fill my lungs with each breath.

The monk shifted ever so slightly, and though his movement was imperceptible, I felt it—a subtle shift in the air—as though he had something to say; as though he had been waiting for me. He opened his eyes and looked directly at me. In that moment, our gazes locked, and I saw a deep understanding in his eyes—one that transcended words.

I sensed a shift in the atmosphere—as though the very walls were holding their breath, waiting for something to be revealed. He opened his hand and showed me a white stone. The stone, inscribed with ancient carvings, appeared worn by time, yet the symbols were still discernible. It depicted a figure—a human body—carved with seven symbols, both familiar and strange.

The monk explained that the white stone was the master key—each symbol symbolized how to open the physical body's seven seals. One by one, from bottom to top, he pointed to the symbols.

Seal #1 is AIR—opens the power of the breath of God.
Seal #2 is FIRE—opens the power of the mind of Christ.
Seal #3 is EARTH—opens the power and purpose of food.
Seal #4 is WATER—opens the power of love.

He paused, taking a breath.

Air—Fire—Earth—Water, he continued, *In the Book of Revelation, they represent the four horsemen of the apocalypse.*

The hidden meaning of the word "apocalypse" signifies a profound unveiling or opening, often involving a shift in understanding or a transformative experience, rather than solely a catastrophic event.

As such...

Only a few—A-F-E-W—will understand the hidden secrets of this code; for it is the Christ Code—the frequency of Light within us that opens the seals.

The other three seals are Sound, Sight, and Spirit.

Seal #5 is SOUND—opens the power of your words.
Seal #6 is SIGHT—opens the power of your imagination.
Seal #7 is SPIRIT—opens the power of your rebirth.

I was baffled. What was this white stone and where did it come from?

The cave, the very air around me, the monk, the white stone, the symbols, the human body, the seven seals—they all became a part of an unfolding mystery.

The silence stretched on. The cave remained still, as if holding its breath, waiting for my mind to catch up with the wisdom I had just received. A shift stirred within me, like a newly planted seed quietly preparing to sprout beneath the soil.

I now understood that opening the seven seals within our physical bodies is a journey we all must take when we're truly ready to shift from a fallen state of physical consciousness to an ascended state of spiritual consciousness, where we finally remember who and what we truly are and were before The Fall.

This is The Return!
This is The Great Awakening!

The monk, ever silent, gazed at me with knowing eyes. His gaze sought neither affirmation nor denial; it simply held space for the awakening unfolding within me. His silence was no longer an absence of sound, but an invitation to listen more deeply—to hear the truths that lay beyond the chatter of the mind.

As I left the cave, I gazed at the rising sun, which bathed the island in a mysterious, candescent golden light. A profound sense of gratitude filled me for the prophetic awakenings I had just received.

In quiet contemplation, I walked down the rocky hill toward the sea, each step grounded in newfound confidence—an understanding that the seven seals of revelation cannot be grasped through religious or intellectual interpretation. They must be unveiled within us; they must be opened; they must be lived.

PROPHETIC AWAKENING #6
The Seven Churches

It was early morning when I made my way toward the cave again, hoping for more prophetic awakenings. The thick fog reminded me how most of us are veiled from seeing and connecting with the truth of who and what we truly are.

When I arrived, the monk was unlocking the gate. We exchanged a silent nod before walking together toward the entrance. He ushered me inside and stood with his head bowed at the cave's door.

Once again, I settled in the spot where Saint John had sat, hoping for another prophetic awakening. After about an hour of quiet meditation with no new insights, I stood for a moment, then began walking toward the exit. The monk nodded as if to dismiss me, but just as I was about to leave, he tapped me on the shoulder.

Moses, he said, introducing himself.

I smiled, unable to resist asking... *like the Moses who parted the Red Sea?*

His smile was unmistakable, even through his thick beard.

Moses is my birthname, he humbly responded. *In my Orthodox tradition, we celebrate our "name day" more than our birthdays. We believe names carry meaning and can reflect one's character and destiny.*

Fascinating, I responded. *So, what does the name Moses mean?*

To be born, he replied, *which signifies a spiritual rebirth when one sheds false beliefs and perceptions and enters a new state of being.*

We walked together down the rocky path toward the sea, the fog lifting as the rising sun dazzled us. Moses motioned for me to sit beside him under a tree. I was awe-struck as he gazed at the sun, as though welcoming its light into his eyes. He encouraged me to do the same, so I did.

Moments later, he opened his hand, and there it was—the white stone!

What is this mysterious stone? I asked.

Moses, gazing at the stone, replied, *have you heard of the philosopher's stone?*

Yes, I answered, *it's a tale about how to turn base metal into gold. Some believe it even has the power to shift mortality into immortality. But it's just a tale, right?*

Moses smiled, then said, *some believe it's just a tale, but for me, it symbolizes the ultimate state of perfection or spiritual purity. Its message reveals our potential to transcend the limitations of the mind, allowing us to shift into a higher state of being through an inner transformation. Ultimately, it carries a transcendental message—how to shift from one state into another.*

So, are you saying that this white stone is the real philosopher's stone? I asked.

Moses shrugged. *The stone was given to me by a very wise monk just before he passed. No one knew his age, but he was very old and very wise. It's made from white alabaster, which symbolizes spiritual purity through transformation. Who knows? The old monk may have carved these symbols himself. Like I said, he was incredibly wise.*

Moses turned the stone over. On the other side were seven other symbols, each aligned with the symbols of the seven seals on the front.

He explained, *the seven churches and the seven seals, as written in revelations, are interconnected. Each church represents a fallen state of consciousness. Here's how the old monk saw it, and how I see it now...*

The seven churches represent seven stages toward spiritual transformation. Each church is linked to an endocrine gland. Endocrine glands produce hormones, which are messengers in the body. So, we should all be asking: What type of messages, through my thoughts and feelings, am I sending to my endocrine glands?

I was so captivated I could hardly breathe.

The first church represents our sex glands. In this sealed spiritual center of light, the message reveals that most of us have lost our connection with our first love—Christ, the light of the world—

who dwells within us. In this fallen state, the illusion of separation triggers a hormonal response, creating a deeply seated need for sex. This consciousness creates a longing to find someone to fill this void, ultimately veiling the sense of oneness.

The key to opening the first seal lies in transcending the illusion of separation through the power of our breath—AIR.

The second church represents our adrenal glands. In this sealed spiritual center of light, the message reveals that most of our minds have been filled with false beliefs and perceptions. In this fallen state, a fiery, fear-driven 'fight or flight' consciousness triggers a hormonal response, creating a survival instinct. This consciousness creates a feeling of scarcity, ultimately veiling the sense of abundance.

The key to opening the second seal lies in transcending the illusion of scarcity by adopting the mind of Christ—FIRE.

The third church represents our pancreas gland. In this sealed spiritual center of light, the message reveals that most of us are trapped in an intellectually driven ego that questions the unseen world. In this fallen state, the need to control triggers a hormonal response, fostering a 'prove it' attitude. This consciousness creates a 'I have to see it to believe it' physical reality, ultimately veiling the unseen world of Spirit.

The key to opening the third seal lies in transcending the ego's 'prove it' attitude by surrendering to the 'all-knowing' who dwells within us all—EARTH.

The fourth church represents our thymus gland. In this sealed spiritual center of light, the message reveals that painful memories of the past have left an impression upon our hearts, making us afraid to love again. In this fallen state, the need to protect our heart triggers a hormonal response, creating an 'I'm not enough' feeling. This consciousness pushes love away, ultimately veiling the power of love.

The key to opening the fourth seal lies in transcending the painful memories of our past by circulating the power of love within our hearts—WATER.

The fifth church represents our thyroid gland. In this sealed spiritual center of light, the message reveals that many of us have used the power of the spoken word unwisely. In this fallen state, we remain unaware that whatever we speak, audibly or silently, following the words—I AM—triggers a hormonal response, creating what we experience. This consciousness creates a feeling of powerlessness, ultimately veiling the creative power of your words.

The key to opening the fifth seal lies in speaking what we want to create, rather than what we don't want, after the words 'I AM,' for I AM is the name of our Creator—SOUND.

The sixth church represents our pineal gland. In this sealed spiritual center of light, the message reveals the power of our imagination through what some call 'the third eye,' and others, the 'single eye.' In this fallen state, most are unaware that the images stored in our subconscious mind from the past, trigger a hormonal response, creating our tomorrows. This consciousness creates a feeling of victimization, ultimately veiling the power of imagination.

The key to opening the sixth seal lies in creating new images and focusing our attention on what we want to experience, as though we have already received it—SIGHT.

The seventh church represents our pituitary gland. In this sealed spiritual center of Light, the message reveals that most of us exist behind a veil of forgetfulness—a state in which we have forgotten that were made in the image and likeness of our Creator. In this fallen state, we have lost awareness of who and what we truly are, which triggers a hormonal response, ultimately veiling our mastery.

Interestingly, the word "sin" means "to forget."

Thus, the key to opening the seventh seal is to cultivate a heightened level of remembering our mastery as we approach the final state of enlightenment—our ultimate union with SPIRIT.

Moses concluded by saying, And when our physical body's seven seals have all been opened, it will truly be "the end of the world as we have always known it to be."

Moses and I exchanged a look with eyes of oneness. The silence between us spoke volumes—a knowing that our paths had been destined to cross. The cave, the revelations, the apocalypse, the shift, the end of time—it all pointed to one truth—our mission was the same: to help people prepare their physical bodies for the shift of the ages—the shift from a fallen state of physical consciousness to an ascended state of spiritual consciousness—the realization that Christ, the Spirit of God, dwells within us.

Ultimately, there is no separation!

PROPHETIC AWAKENING #7
The New Earth

Moses excused himself with a graceful nod and walked back up the hill toward the cave. I remained seated on the rocky terrain in silence, reflecting on everything he had just shared. Hearing from an Orthodox monk that Christ, the Spirit of God, dwells within us—and not just in some far-off place called Heaven—shifted me forever, confirming what I had shown years earlier.

A wave of sadness filled my heart as I realized that our suffering is rooted in this false belief—the belief that we're separate from God, nature, and from everything and everyone around us. This false belief in consciousness is indeed, our only problem.

My new eyes fixed on the sun peeking over the blue waters of the Aegean Sea. Suddenly, a butterfly landed on my knee. I began recalling how a lowly caterpillar could possibly transform itself into a beautiful butterfly, such as this one.

Much like our own transformation, a caterpillar undergoes metamorphosis, where hormones trigger the release of enzymes that break down its tissues, allowing for rebirth to take place—but only when its body is ready. In essence, like us, caterpillars have an endocrine system that produces hormones, which not only regulate every aspect of their lives but also facilitate their final state of transformation.

The next morning, I anxiously walked toward the cave. I felt a wave of gratitude when I saw that the gate was cracked open. Moses greeted me with his usual silent nod at the cave's entrance and ushered me inside—this time, with an ear-to-ear grin.

I sat down in my usual spot, praying for one last prophetic awakening before returning to the States the next day. Moments later, I was captivated as I watched the Angelic Presence appear. Its golden halo of light descended above the crown of my head—the location of the seventh seal. No words were spoken. Instead, I had a vision of the New Earth.

As I closed my eyes, I saw...

> *An earth within the earth—like a universe within the universe. This New Earth is emerging. Its waters are holy, streaming through towns and cities, and when we drink of this living water, we never die. For it holds the eternal code of life.*
>
> *It's a place without suffering—a place where the tree of life offers us its fruit—a place where the air is celestial, the light eternal, and the day without night. It's a place where people love each other as themselves—a place that could only be called Heaven on Earth.*

Our physical bodies must be made ready, for in this vibrant new world, fear and death have lost their hold.

And in the twinkling of an eye, our mortal bodies will become bodies of light—the body that once died will now forever live.

Blessed are you who are prepared to enter. Only one question remains… are you ready?

The time has come.
The time to prepare our physical bodies for the shift of the ages is now.
The New Earth Fast is how!

– 2 –
SHIFT WITH THE NEW MOON
Blood–Our Inner Red Sea

A few days before the new moon, I packed my bags and headed east to a friend's vacant condo on the Atlantic coast of Florida to fast and meditate for seven days. I was determined to do whatever it took to prepare my physical body for the shift of the ages.

Having been back in the States for about a month, I craved solitude. I needed time alone to fully surrender myself to the surge of the ocean tides, letting their ebb and flow wash over me and assist in releasing any false beliefs and perceptions that had long veiled my body's seven seals.

The next morning, I walked down to the beach and squished my toes into the wet sand. The sun was just beginning to rise, so, like Moses, I sat down and gazed at the glorious hues of the sky. But then, I smelled the most noxious, almost unbearable odor. When I looked around, I could hardly believe my eyes—dead fish were everywhere!

I was shocked, and at the same time, it felt serendipitous. It was as though something monumental was stirring in my mind—Red Tide, the Red Sea. The Red Sea, normally blue-green, may have acquired its name because of a similar red-tide phenomenon—an overgrowth of algae that, when it dies off, turns the seawater reddish-brown.

The night before, I had been thinking about Moses and how he believed the entire Bible, when not taken literally, was a story of salvation rather than secular history—that every character, from Adam to Eve, to Moses, to Jesus, to Mary Magdalene, represents states of consciousness within us all, as signified by their names.

I became intrigued by the story of the Red Sea and how Moses parted it to free the children of Israel from bondage under the rule of the Egyptian Pharaoh, guiding them toward the Promised Land. So, if Moses of Patmos is correct, how does the Exodus story unfold within our consciousness?

With that thought, I walked back to the condo, where I could sit on the balcony and gaze at the sun as it continued its ascent over the water's edge, distant and free from the stench of the dying algae and fish. My head and heart, much like the sun and the moon, were facing each other. Everything inside me felt unstable, unsure of almost everything—the future of our planet, the future of humanity. How do we create change in the world when everything appeared to be such a mess? A massive war had just broken out in Kuwait.

Even though my heart longed to enter the Promised Land—a state of spiritual fulfillment—I felt as though I, along with all of humanity, was still living in Egyptian times, in bondage to a patriarchal, male-driven governmental system whose controlling dictatorship was blooming (like algae) out of control. We were no longer America the Free.

As I stood facing the rising sun, the turbulent waters of my mind became very, very still. A few moments later, I felt the Angelic Presence all around me, saying...

> *You came into this life to free your soul. Freedom is the opposite of bondage, which was once imposed upon the children of Israel.*
>
> *You came into this life to learn that you are neither male nor female, black nor white, Jewish nor Gentile.*
>
> *You chose your body, and your family was chosen by you for this great purpose also. You must learn to love your father's patriarchal, controlling, male ego, for he has truly been your greatest learning tool of all while you have been in the earthly plane.*
>
> *You must learn to love what you have been blessed with.*
>
> *Isn't it also interesting that you had four male brothers who surrounded you as you were growing up? After some thought, does that surprise you?*
>
> *Again, the thing to meditate on day and night is that you are neither male nor female. You are Pure Spirit—Spirit who is FREE—free to be the ultimate in anything that you choose to do.*
>
> *To achieve freedom for your soul, you must learn to love your feminine being; to cherish her; to caress her every trait. You must learn to have a loving relationship with yourself, as that is truly all you are ever having.*

For everything and everyone who becomes a part of your life is simply there for your learning. When you learn to look deep within the mirror, seeing only your reflection, then and only then will you be able to delve deeper into the heart of your very own soul.

For you are and always have been a great crusader and a healer of souls. You set my people free; you turned them out of bondage. But look, don't you see, my people are still in bondage; they are not free even now.

Since the beginning of time, people have always looked outside of themselves for a savior. Jesus was the greatest savior of all, yet people continue to look outside of themselves to be set free.

Your freedom message to yourself and to all beings during this life is not America the Free! But it's Freedom for the Soul, for as each soul is free, America will be free!

To achieve freedom for the soul, you must focus your attention on the great I AM THAT I AM that you know of, and understand that THIS is your power, and it lives within you as it does within everyone around you.

Know that nothing lies between you and your Creator, absolutely nothing! Then, as you do this great work, others will simply follow.

So, quit looking outside of yourself for a savior to come and save you. For you must learn to love, honor, and revere the savior that's already within.

You, and all of humanity, are magnificent creations of the Divine!

After hearing this profound message about how to free our souls through the power of the great "I AM THAT I AM," my mind became consumed with the story of Exodus.

I became fascinated by how each character and location in the Exodus story mirrors the shifting apocalyptic times we're living in—shifting from bondage to freedom, from our fallen state of physical consciousness to an ascended state of spiritual consciousness. Though this journey has been arduous for me so far, it is one we must all take when we are ready to free our souls from the illusionary bondage of physical consciousness and remember once again who and what we truly are—Pure Spirit!

Exodus–Freedom For Your Soul

One of the earliest stories that references the sign of our times is found in the book of Exodus. This is the story of the Israelites—their bondage and slavery in Egypt under the tyrannical rule of Pharaoh—and their eventual deliverance by God through the prophet Moses.

In this great story, we witness Pharaoh's hardened heart as he refused to free the Israelites from slavery. Moses warned Pharaoh that God would smite Egypt if he did not release them, but Pharaoh refused to listen.

Ten plagues swept throughout the land of Egypt—each one a consequence of Pharaoh's hardened heart and his refusal to set the children of Israel free. But finally, after the death of his firstborn son, Pharaoh realized that the God of Moses—the great I AM—was more powerful than the gods he worshipped, and so, he reluctantly released them.

Moses then led the children of Israel out of Egypt through a desolate wilderness toward the Promised Land. However, shortly after their departure, Pharaoh had a change of heart and sent his army after them. The Israelites, fearing for their lives, lost faith. Trapped between Pharaoh's army behind them and the sea ahead of them, Moses parted the waters of the Red Sea, allowing the Israelites to cross safely. In that moment, their faith was restored.

Throughout the ages, nothing has really changed, other than the characters, locations, and the unique ways in which ruling governmental systems and human consciousness have played out around the world.

I asked myself...

- Could the story of Exodus and the Israelites departure from slavery in Egypt signify our own transformative liberation?
- Could it be that there are hidden gems within this great story to show us how to become a free, sovereign people, governed by the great I AM THAT I AM—gems that hold the key to free us from our fallen state of physical consciousness—gems that frees our soul from the limitations of our human mind that hinder us from becoming all we were created to be?
- Could it be that the seven seals and seven churches (endocrine glands) are interconnected within the Exodus story?
- Could it be that once we shift our seven fallen states of physical consciousness, and our physical body's seven seals have all been opened, the consciousness of our world will also shift?

- Could it truly be that to change the world, we must first change ourselves?

Mahatma Gandhi, one of India's greatest political and spiritual leaders who pioneered and practiced resistance to tyranny through mass nonviolent civil disobedience, said...

> *"We but mirror the world. All the tendencies present in the outer world are to be found in the world of our body. If we could change ourselves, the tendencies in the world would also change. As a man changes his own nature, so does the attitude of the world change towards him."*

If we were to entertain the possibility that each character within the story of Exodus might just represent an archetypal quality that continues to play itself out in our psyches—that there really is no past or future—my question then becomes, how do we break free from the bonds that keep us enslaved so we can live our lives as free, sovereign souls?

Afterall, the word Exodus signifies a liberation from bondage or oppression, whether physical or spiritual, and a journey towards a new, promised state of freedom and purpose.

Pharaoh, Moses, and the Israelites

Our Exodus (to exit) journey begins by exploring Exodus's two main characters: Pharaoh and Moses. Again, rather than merely seeing them as historical characters, let's view them as a portrayal of two opposing aspects of our own consciousness, and how they're being played out in our world today.

Pharaoh characterizes our Ego-Mind—the part of our mind that sees everything and everyone through the eyes of the physical world, thus seeing through the eyes of separation, which creates a false sense of self- identity. Once caught up in a false-self-identity, a type of self-centeredness takes hold whose focus is on self-interest, material gain and greed. This false identity is the EGO, the part of our mind that has Edged God Out and, therefore, needs to be in control. Ego is the Latin word for "I." It's the "me-my-I" attitude that not only disconnects us from the great I AM THAT I AM, but it also triggers the sense of fear, pride, envy, lust, greediness, gluttony, and anger, which in turn creates a weakened immune system that ultimately causes sickness, disease, and death!

The Ego-Mind, caught up in the five senses, material-driven physical world, with its ego-identity, might tell you...

I AM physical.
I AM a democrat.
I AM a republican.
I AM Jewish.
I AM Christian.
I AM a Muslim.
I AM Buddhist.
I AM Hindu.
I AM Greek.

I AM Mexican.
I AM English.
I AM American.
I AM Asian.
I AM Russian.
I AM white.
I AM black.
I AM male.
I AM female.

This Ego-Mind may also tell you…

> I AM sick.
> I AM fat.
> I AM ugly.
> I AM broke.
> I AM stupid.
>
> I AM afraid.
> I AM worthless.
> I AM not enough.
> I AM a victim.
> I AM guilty.

These false sense of self ego-identities keep us veiled from who and what we truly are. They keep us enslaved to false beliefs and perceptions… all of which creates division and wars with one another, keeping us caught up in our ego's need to be in control. Our greatest challenge is to break free from our Pharaoh-type Ego-Mind—the mind that hardens our heart and creates our suffering—the mind that has held us in bondage to the physical world for way too long!

The time to shift out of the old and into the new is now—the shift from the fallen state of physical consciousness that keeps us in bondage to the Ego-Mind so we can shift into the ascended state of spiritual consciousness of the Spirit-Mind!

Moses characterizes our Spirit-Mind—the part of our mind that sees everything and everyone through the eyes of the spiritual world, thus seeing through the eyes of oneness, which creates a selfless identity. The Spirit-Mind lives in the non-physical, unseen world of Spirit whose selfless identity is focused on "we" and what's good for the whole. It's the Spirit-Mind's "we-us-our" attitude that creates love, compassion, peace, patience, kindness, and faith, which ultimately creates a dynamic immunity and a long, healthy, prosperous life on Earth as it is in Heaven!

The Spirit-Mind, caught up in the ascended spiritual world, with its selfless Spirit identity, will tell you...

I AM Pure Spirit.
I AM one with God.
I AM one with nature.
I AM one with everyone.
I AM full of faith.
I AM perfect.
I AM in perfect health.
I AM my perfect body weight.
I AM vibrant.
I AM full of energy.
I AM wealthy.
I AM a powerful creator.
I AM a master.
I AM grateful.
I AM safe
I AM peaceful.
I AM kind.
I AM love.
I AM free.
I AM eternal.

Once we realize that we are, in fact, Pure Spirit, is when our physical bodies will become "Spirit-filled"... and the moment that our souls will once again become free from the bondage of physical consciousness that keeps us in bondage to sickness, disease, and death!

This is because...

In Spirit, there is no disease.
In Spirit, there is no time.
In Spirit, there is only oneness.
In Spirit, there is no suffering.
In Spirit, there is no sickness.
In Spirit, there is no aging.
In Spirit, there is no fear.
In Spirit, nothing can harm us.
In Spirit, we are immune to everything.

Because God's Spirit doesn't live in time, the Spirit-Mind can only speak in the present moment, as though what you're speaking, silently or audibly, has already happened! Knowing and practicing these attitudes on a moment-by-moment basis will, therefore, set you free from the slavery of the Ego-Mind's self-serving clutches and change the course of your life forever!

Israelites represent the illumined thoughts of our soul, which have fallen into the wilderness of the physical world and is crying out to be set from the captivity of physical consciousness. In the beginning of our soul's journey from physical consciousness to spiritual consciousness—from our Pharaoh, Ego-Mind to our Moses, Spirit-Mind—such a journey may feel hopeless at times; that Pharaoh, the Ego-Mind, has such a hold on us, that it may never let us go. It has received false impressions from the outer egoistic world and has taken on thoughts of limitations.

These doubting, fearful, limiting thoughts represent Pharaoh's army.

But when we turn our consciousness away from the limitations of the physical world and realize that we are more Spirit than physical, our soul will once again be set free from the bondage of physical consciousness, which results in the spiritualization of our physical bodies.

Egypt and the Promised Land

Our Exodus journey continues by exploring Egypt and the Promised Land—not merely as historical places, but as two distinct "lands" within the human body.

Egypt is located within the upper and lower regions of our abdomen, often referred to as the gut. It represents the area where the Ego-Mind

(Pharaoh) resides. It is the place where the "me-my-I" ego seeks control, where the still small voice of Spirit cannot be heard. It is a space driven by the physical world, characterized by greed, material gain, and an insatiable appetite that can never be satisfied. Here, the "plagues of Egypt" manifest—symbolizing the suffering and afflictions that bind our souls to sickness, disease, and death.

Thus, the maxim...

"Death begins in the colon!"

However, it is also the place where our greatest transformation can occur. It is where the ego, in its self-centered identity, must relinquish its need to control. It is here that the ego surrenders to the guidance of the Spirit-Mind, walking side by side toward the Promised Land.

The Promised Land is located within the region of the heart. It represents the space within us where the Spirit-Mind resides—the place where the "we-us-our" voice of Spirit can be heard. In this sacred space, the focus shifts from self to love and the matters of the heart. It's here that the great, I AM THAT I AM takes hold within us, freeing our souls from the fear-driven slavery of the Pharaoh (the Ego-Mind). In this place, our inner Moses—the Spirit-Mind—parts the Red Sea within, leading us to live a long, healthy, and prosperous life within the Promised Land of our hearts.

Thus, the maxim...

"Blessed are the pure in heart for they shall see God!"

The Wilderness and the Red Sea
Even though the Israelites had left Egypt, the slave mentality still lingered in their consciousness. As individuals and as a collective, they couldn't enter the Promised Land until they had complete trust and faith in the great, I AM THAT I AM.

Their struggle to have faith in an unseen God was deep, which likely explains why they built the golden calf. It wasn't until the entire generation of Israelites who had lived under slavery in Egypt had died—symbolizing the release of fearful thoughts and false perceptions—that they regained their faith. Only then were they finally free to cross the Red Sea and enter the Promised Land.

The Wilderness represents the place within us where we wander, feeling separate from Spirit. It's where the Ego-Mind and the Spirit-Mind are in a constant tug-of-war. In this place, our faith in the unseen world of Spirit wavers, and we often feel as though we'll never be free from the grip of the Pharaoh Ego-Mind that keeps our souls in bondage to fear—and ultimately, sickness, disease, and death.

Living in the Promised Land often feels more like a dream than a reality. We wander in the wilderness of life, tossed back and forth between these two opposing forces, until the moment arrives when our Ego-Mind surrenders completely to the guidance of Spirit—the great, I AM THAT I AM—who resides within each of us. It is at this moment that our faith in the unseen world of Spirit is restored. It is then we can truly say...

"Thy will be done!"

The Red Sea represents our blood. Blood is a rich, scarlet soup that transports oxygen and nutrients to every cell of our body. Thus, the saying "life is in the blood" holds deep significance.

Some religious traditions believe that the blood of animals should never be eaten for this reason—that blood is the seat of the soul. This is the main reason the Jewish tradition drains the blood of an animal before eating, thus the Kosher seal. Some belief systems also hold that blood radiates light, connecting our physical bodies to Spirit and serving as a gateway between the physical and spiritual worlds.

The crossing of the Red Sea (our blood), therefore, symbolizes our redemption, deliverance, and liberation from the false belief that we are merely a physical body. It awakens us to the truth that we are, in fact, Pure Spirit!

This apocalyptic Exodus journey marks our personal Passover—a journey from the Ego-Mind to the Spirit-Mind—a journey from plagues to the miraculous. It's a journey that lifts the veil between the physical and spiritual worlds, opening the book of seven seals within our physical body. It marks the end of the world as we have known it and ushers us into a transcendent world of our true selves.

This is The Return!

The time has come.
The time to PASSOVER is now.
The New Earth Fast is how!

– 3 –
THE POWER OF THE NEW MOON FAST
Our Body's Internal Waterways

To prepare for your personal Passover, it is imperative to have a more in-depth understanding of the power of cleansing your body, mind, and soul during the 7-day new moon phase. Radiating an air of mystery and magic, the moon has long been associated with dreamtime and the art of healing. In ancient times, adepts used the cycles of the moon to not only measure time, but to regulate the healing of the sick and the mentally insane. These mystical adepts understood the power of moon cycles and believed that they create a gateway of both destruction—the breaking down of the old—and creation—the resurrection of the new.

Moon Phases
How They Affect Water

The term "moon cycle," also known as the lunar cycle, refers to the moon's continuous orbit around the Earth. To complete one full orbit, the moon takes about 29.5 days—from new moon to new moon. As we observe the moon from Earth, it appears to wax, or grow larger, until it becomes a glowing silver-white disk. Then, it begins to wane, or shrink, until it forms a crescent sliver before vanishing altogether for a few days. The changing appearance of the moon provides us with a clear indication of its progress.

The new moon phase begins when the sun and moon are in alignment, facing each other. This is why the moon is not visible in the sky during this phase, and it's sometimes referred to as the "dark moon." The day after the new moon, the moon begins to grow again, entering an endless cycle of light and dark that repeats over and over.

Each lunation consists of approximately four 7-day moon phases: the new moon, first quarter, full moon, and last (or third) quarter moon.

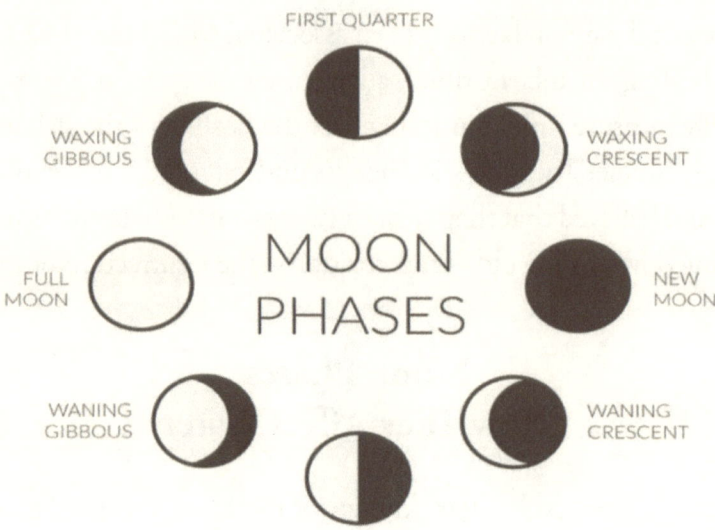

The moon is the Earth's closest celestial neighbor. Its gravitational pull—a magnetic tug between the moon and the Earth—affects ocean tides and currents, which in turn influence shifting weather and climate patterns. The moon's pull on Earth causes ocean tides to rise (as water moves onto land) and fall (as water moves away from land). Its gravitational effect is so strong that it literally pulls the vast oceanic waters into a bulge on the side of Earth facing the moon. The centrifugal force, generated by Earth's rotation, also creates a bulge on the opposite side. As a result, there are approximately two high and low tides each day.

However, what many are unaware of is that the moon's gravitational pull on Earth's waters also exerts a pull on the waters of our physical bodies. After all, we are made up of approximately 75 percent water, much like our planet.

> *"Water is the driving force of all nature."*
> –Leonardo Da Vinci

Our Body's Internal Waterways

As previously stated, our physical bodies are made up primarily of water, just like planet Earth. Much like the trillions of fish that swim in the waters of our Earth, we have trillions of cells that "swim" through the waters of our body. Most of our cells move through miles of tube-like tributaries, such as arteries, vessels, veins, and capillaries—our body's "internal waterways."

These waterways branch out much like the rivers of Earth, as seen in the following two images. Our blood vessels even resemble the tributaries of a river.

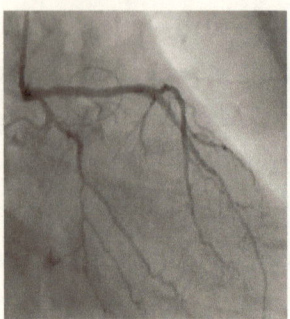 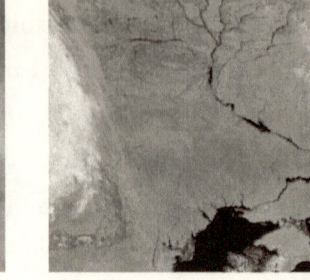

X-ray of blood vessels   Arial view of branches of a river

These visual images should serve as a constant reminder of how wondrously and magnificently we are made. They also reflect how our physical body mirrors the planetary body.

Our Earth has two distinctive types of waterways—freshwater and saltwater—through which water circulates. In the same way, our physical body has two main circulatory systems—cardiovascular and lymphatic—through which blood and lymph circulate.

As we explore these two vast waterways in our body, there are two key questions to ask ourselves:

(1) How does the gravitational pull of the moon, especially during the 7-day new moon phase, affect our body's two internal waterways?

(2) How does fasting, forgiveness, and prayer during the 7-day new moon phase promote a strong immune system?

Our Body's Two Vast Waterways
Blood and Lymph

If you were to examine the human body under a high-powered microscope, you would see nothing more than trillions of cells and two major fluids—blood and lymph.

The cardiovascular system circulates blood, while the lymphatic system circulates lymph. Though both systems are circulatory in nature, they work separately to perform distinct functions.

The key difference between these two fluids is their function:

- Blood carries nutrients, hormones, and oxygen through the circulatory system to the trillions of cells that make up our organs, glands, bones, and tissues.
- Lymph removes cellular waste through the lymphatic system. It transports waste to the lymph nodes through a network of lymph vessels, where it is held before being eliminated from the body via the kidneys.

In essence, the lymphatic system is a complex network of vessels, ducts, lymph nodes, spleen, thymus, adenoids, and tonsils that cleanses our internal ecosystem. It collects toxins, bacteria, and even cancer cells. Interestingly, the lymphatic system is two-and-a-half to three times larger than the entire circulatory (blood) system!

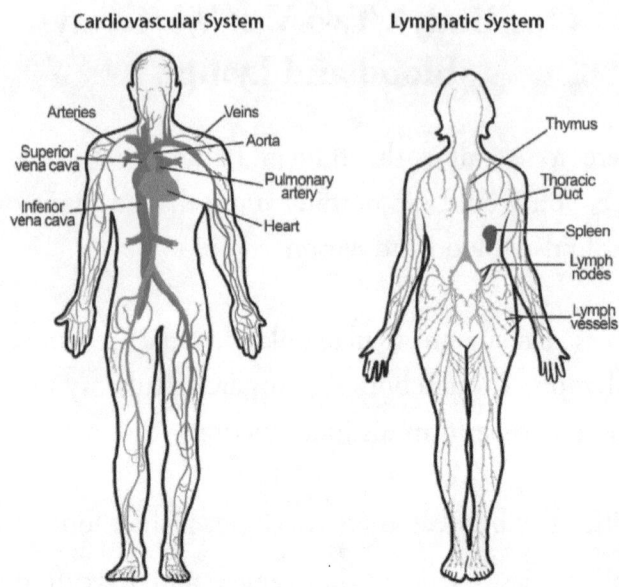

Functions of Blood:

Blood plays a critical role in the body's cardiovascular system, performing various functions such as:

- Regulating body temperature.
- Regulating the water content of the cells.
- Protecting against excess blood loss through clotting.
- Regulating pH by interacting with acids and alkalis.
- Transporting hormones, nutrients, enzymes, respiratory gases, and other molecules to the respective parts of the body.

Functions of Lymph:

Lymph performs essential functions within the lymphatic system, including:

- Removing metabolic waste from tissue cells.
- Maintaining the composition of tissue fluid.

- Guarding the entry of pathogenic infections caused by microbes.
- Absorbing fat-soluble vitamins and other digested fat molecules from the small intestines through lymphatic vessels.

Throughout the day, our cells are continually producing waste as a by-product of metabolism. After absorbing nutrients from the blood, metabolic waste is released into the lymphatic vessels. The lymph nodes filter this waste, and the filtered lymph then travels to lymphatic ducts, where it is returned to the blood. It's as if there's a higher intelligence orchestrating a symbiotic, two-step circulatory dance between these two great systems—the cardiovascular system, which distributes nutrients, and the lymphatic system, which eliminates waste.

These two fluids are the dance of life within us. One system is constantly giving, and the other is receiving and releasing.

> Cardiovascular system: Nutrients in!
> Lymphatic system: Waste out!

For these two waterways to remain in perfect health, their circulation must be unobstructed. Proper circulation is critical to cellular health, as is maintaining the pH balance of these vast fluid systems.

Blood and Lymph pH

A holistically minded medical perspective is emerging today: disease is intimately related to the pH of the fluids in our body. Virtually every degenerative disease—such as cancer, heart disease, joint pain, osteoporosis, arthritis, and neurological conditions—along with skin disorders and even tooth decay, have been directly associated with an excess of acid in the body's tissues and fluids.

In chemistry, pH means, potential of hydrogen, which measures the acidity or alkalinity of a water-based fluid. The pH scale runs from 0 to 14:

- A pH of 7 is neutral (neither acid nor alkaline).
- Fluids with a pH lower than 7 are acidic—the lower the number, the more acidic.
- Fluids with a pH higher than 7 are alkaline—the higher the number, the more alkaline.

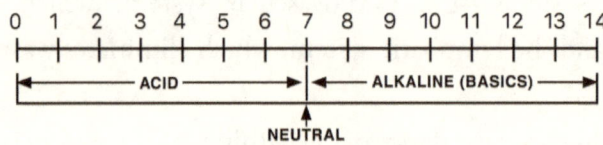

The pH Scale

The pH measurement of a fluid is directly related to the amount of oxygen it contains—the higher the pH reading, the more oxygen—the lower the pH reading, the less oxygen. Within the human body, our fluids should have a pH measurement of approximately 7.35-7.4, which equates to an oxygenated environment. If, however, the pH measurement of our fluids should drop below 7, a low-oxygenated environment ensues—the lower the drop, the lower the oxygen levels become.

Aerobic bacteria (or aerobes) are beneficial (good) bacteria that flourish in an oxygen-rich environment, whereas anaerobic bacteria are unbeneficial (bad) bacteria that flourish in a low-oxygen environment.

This is the KEY to understanding the power of pH and how we thrive and how we become sick and die!

In short, if our body's interstitial fluids—the fluids that our cells "swim" in—are slightly alkaline (7.35-7.4) and oxygen-rich, our cells and beneficial bacteria thrive, as do we! But if our body's interstitial fluids become acidic (5.5-6.5) and oxygen-starved, our cells and beneficial bacteria become sick and die, as do we!

When enough of our cells and beneficial bacteria die, unbeneficial bacteria become the dominant force that sets the stage for almost every disease known. If this is allowed to happen, our bodies will painfully and slowly be reduced back into the dust of the earth!.

Think about the pH value of water in your hot tub or swimming pool. Checking its pH is crucial because if it drops below 7, it fosters the growth of unfriendly bacteria—the water becomes green with algae. The pump (just like the heart) that circulates the water becomes clogged, leading to clogged arteries.

Maintaining the proper pH balance within the waters of our body is, therefore, the key to a happy, healthy, sustainable life.

Our Cardiovascular System

Our cardiovascular system consists of the heart and the blood vessels that run throughout the entire body. Arteries carry blood away from the heart, while veins return it. The network of blood vessels is like a branching system of rivers, with the main artery (aorta) branching into smaller arteries, which then divide into even smaller vessels.

The smallest arteries end in a network of tiny vessels known as the capillary network.

The heart has four chambers: the left atrium, right atrium, right ventricle, and left ventricle. Our eight pints of blood, which I figuratively call the "river of life," circulates through the entire cardiovascular system about 60 times an hour, absorbing oxygen from the lungs and passing through the heart, which then pumps this oxygen-rich blood outward.

Interestingly, one morning during meditation, I had another prophetic awakening. I saw that the flow of blood through these four chambers mirrored the "four rivers of Eden!"

> *"A river flowed out of Eden to water the garden, and there it divided and became four rivers."*
> -Genesis 2: 10

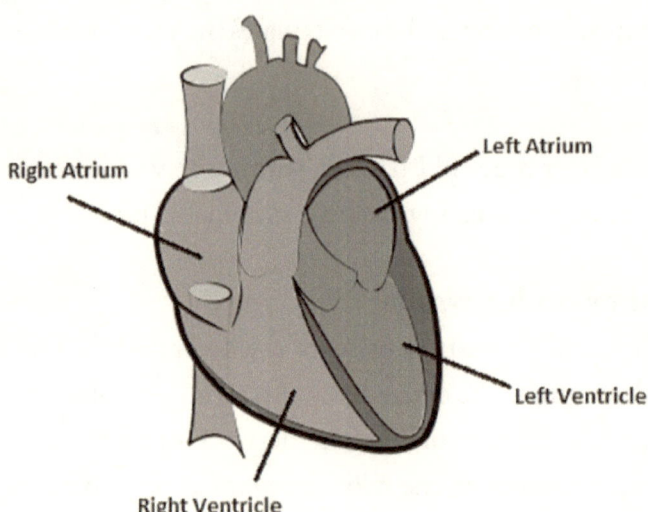

Like the four rivers of Eden, these four chambers are separated by one-way valves that regulate the direction of blood flow. As the heart pumps blood, these valves open and close tightly, ensuring the blood flows in only one direction, just as the rivers of Eden divided and flowed outward. just like the four rivers of Eden! The vision was quite a revelation!

Take a moment and ask yourself...

- Could it be that before The Fall, we lived in the "inner earth"—the Garden of Eden—the place where our consciousness was fully connected with God, nature, and everything and everyone who only appeaars to be outside of us?
- Could it be that after The Fall, we were sent to the "outer earth," where our consciousness shifted into a "false world of appearance," causing us to perceive everything, including God, as separate from us?
- Could it be that the Garden of Eden exists within our hearts, where our consciousness (the garden) perceives its oneness with God, nature, and everyone (paradise), who only "appears" to be outside of us?
- Could it be that when we fast, forgive, and pray during the 7-day new moon phase—when the moon's gravitational pull on the waters (our blood) is at its peak—we have the potential to purify our hearts, returning us to our original state of being?

"Blessed are the pure in heart, for they will see God."
–Matthew 5:8

The *New Moon Fast* not only cleanses the body of toxins, but it also purifies our hearts of false beliefs and perceptions.

To clarify...

> The 7-day new moon phase is when the moon's gravitational pull on the waters of our bodies is strongest. During this time, the viscosity (tension) of our blood relaxes, opening the way for toxic waste, as well as false beliefs and perceptions, to be released, allowing us to remember who we truly are.
>
> This is The Return!

Consider this...

- The name Moses means: To be born, to draw out, to extract, or remove from water.
- The Red Sea (blood) represents: A sea of false beliefs and perceptions.
- The Promised Land represents: The Return!

Thousands of years before scientists understood the extraordinary life-sustaining properties of blood, scripture told us that "life is in the blood!" This is not only because blood is vital for every cell in our body, but also because it is considered by some to be the very "life force" of God, who lives, moves, and has His being within us.

Thus, maintaining nutrient and oxygen-rich blood that can circulate freely throughout the cardiovascular system is one of the best ways we can prepare our physical bodies for the shift of the ages.

Our Lymphatic System

While the cardiovascular system has been extensively studied by medical science, the lymphatic system has been less understood. However, scientists are now recognizing it as a crucial part of our body's health.

The lymphatic system is a highly sophisticated network of vessels, ducts, lymph nodes, and organs like the spleen, thymus, adenoids, and tonsils. It plays a vital role in filtering out toxins and producing lymphocytes (a type of white blood cell) and other immune cells that destroy bacteria, viruses, parasites, and fungi.

This highlights the importance of ensuring that the lymphatic system circulates freely without obstructions.

- A clean, free-flowing, alkaline lymphatic system = strong immunity.
- A clogged, acidic lymphatic system = weak immunity.
- A weak immunity = sickness, pain, and disease.

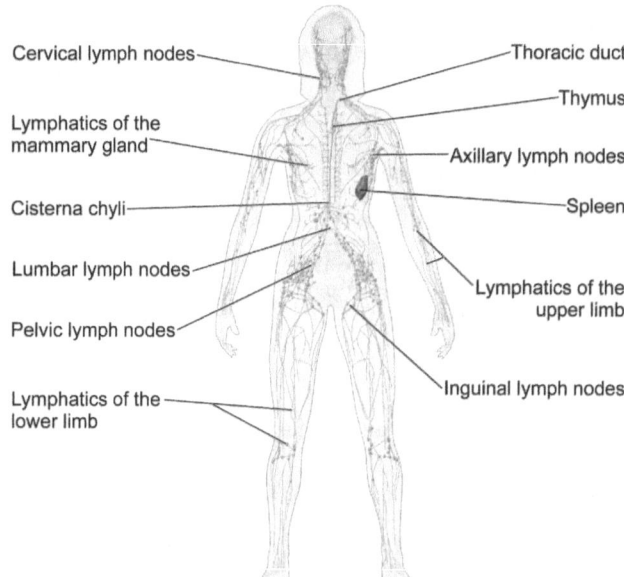

In Greek, the word *lymph* means "pure stream."

Question...

> But what happens if your lymph, instead of being a pure stream, becomes a toxic, stagnant, acidic stream and is unable to circulate properly?

Answer...

> Just like clogged arteries, blocked lymphatic vessels make it difficult for lymph to flow and perform its function properly.

Professor Arnold Ehret (July 29, 1866 – October 10, 1922), author of *Mucusless Diet Healing System*, said,

> *"Every disease, no matter what name it is known by Medical Science, is constipation—a clogging up of the entire pipe system of the human body. Any special symptom is, therefore, merely an extraordinary local constipation by accumulated mucus at this particular place."*

Consider that your lymphatic vessels function like a giant drainage system that must remain open for smooth circulation. Like the drains in your home, if your lymphatic vessels are clogged, waste gets pushed back through your "drains" and spills into your organs, glands, and tissues.

Dr. Robert Morse, author of *The Detox Miracle Sourcebook*, compares the lymphatic system to a sewer system, where waste is transported into lymphatic vessels (like sewer pipes), then carried into lymph nodes (like septic tanks) where immune cells break it down.

He believes that 99 percent of our diseases result from a toxic, acidic, backed-up lymphatic system, which creates an environment for harmful microorganisms to flourish.

Like Dr. Morse, I have come to believe that the trillions of cells in our body can only be as healthy as the fluids they are swimming in.

So, if your organs, glands, or tissues aren't functioning properly, and a disease has been diagnosed, it's possible that you're not sick—you're clogged!

> Dis: to move away from.
> Ease: the natural flow of life.

Lymphatic Vessels and Neurological Diseases

The recent discovery of lymphatic vessels in the brain marks a pivotal shift in understanding the role of the lymphatic system not just in immune response and waste removal throughout the body, but also within the brain—a central organ to our physical and mental health.

The link between the lymphatic system and neurological diseases such as Alzheimer's, dementia, multiple sclerosis, and meningitis underscores the importance of proper lymphatic drainage for brain health. Just as the lymphatic system plays a crucial role in clearing toxins and waste from the rest of the body, its function in the brain appears to be equally critical.

Interestingly, they have also recently discovered that boosting the brain's waste removal improved overall brain health, including memory.

When the lymphatic system in the brain doesn't drain effectively, harmful substances, bacteria (like Chlamydia), fungi, and the buildup of oxidative stress and inflammation can wreak havoc, potentially leading to neurodegenerative conditions.

This discovery aligns with the holistic understanding of body systems being intricately connected—particularly how cleansing and maintaining the health of these systems (through practices like fasting, prayer, and forgiveness) could help mitigate such issues, fostering better brain health and overall wellbeing.

Gut Microbiome and Brain Health

Remember the saying, "death begins in the colon" from Chapter 2? Interestingly, recent scientific research has connected the dots between our gut microbiome—the trillions of bacteria and other microorganisms that reside in the gastrointestinal tract—and our brain health.

The interaction between our gut microbiome and brain health is as follows:

- **Neurotransmitters:**
  Gut bacteria produce neurotransmitters, such as serotonin and dopamine, which can directly influence brain function and mood.
- **Hormones:**
  Microbes can also produce hormones, such as oxytocin, that affect brain activity and social behavior.
- **Immune System:**

The gut microbiome interacts with the immune system, which can send signals to the brain and influence inflammation levels.

- **Blood-Brain Barrier:**
  Gut bacteria can produce metabolites that affect the permeability of the blood-brain barrier, allowing certain substances to cross into the brain.

- **Neurological Disorders:**
  Alterations in the gut microbiome have been linked to neurodegenerative diseases, such as Alzheimer's and Parkinson's, as well as neuropsychiatric disorders, such as depression and anxiety.

- **Cognitive Function:**
  A healthy gut microbiome is associated with improved cognitive function, including memory, attention, and learning.

- **Mood Regulation:**
  Gut bacteria produce neurotransmitters that contribute to mood regulation and can reduce stress levels.

- **Brain Development:**
  The gut microbiome plays a role in brain development during early life, and imbalances can lead to developmental disorders.

Incorporating this knowledge into our understanding of fasting and its role in detoxifying the lymphatic system becomes even more relevant. By promoting the drainage of toxins, reducing inflammation, and allowing the body's natural systems to work at their optimal levels, we support not only physical vitality but also the health of our mind and spirit.

The Internal Acid Rain Theory

As I reflected on the laboratory findings, I began to consider a potential underlying cause for the observed issues.

Consider this...

The brain is encased in water, and the pH of this fluid should range between 7.35 and 7.4. What if the cause of every neurological disease is simply an overly acidic condition, akin to an internal acid rain? For perspective, acid rain has a pH of approximately 5.5.

Acidification leads to oxidative stress (free radical activity) and inflammation—what medical science calls "brain on fire," where the brain becomes inflamed, often accompanied by a burning sensation.

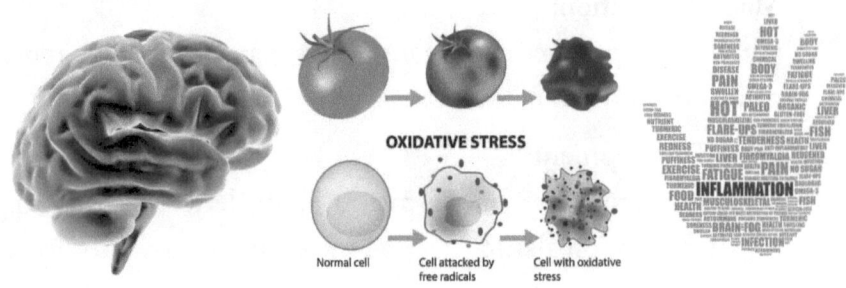

Now consider that...

> Your central nervous system (your brain and spinal column) is much like a tree. Some call it, "the tree of life," but sadly, it can also become, "the tree of death!"

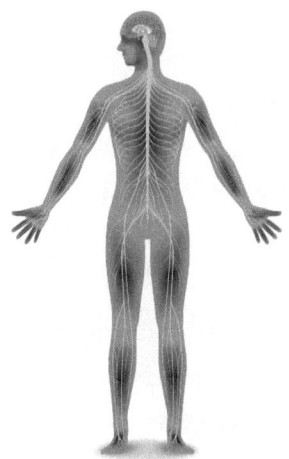

Now consider...

- Like a tree has bark as an outer covering, we have skin.
- Like a tree has a trunk, we have a torso which houses our spinal column.
- Like a tree has branches that are covered with a waxy protective covering to shield it from any type of environmental threat, we have nerves that are covered with a waxy protective layer of fat called the myelin sheath to shield them from any type of environmental threat. This protective covering is essential to a tree's immunity, as well as being essential to our body's immunity.

Sadly, when acid rain falls on a tree, it breaks down the protective coating, leading to oxidation—a process that destroys the structural integrity of the tree. The tree's immunity begins to weaken as the protective coating erodes.

In the same way, internal acid rain can damage the myelin sheath around our nerves, weakening the body's immunity and setting the stage for neurological diseases.

Like a tree has a root system, we have a root system: our intestinal tract. Just as a tree's roots have fine hairs for nutrient absorption, our intestines have villi—tiny hairs that absorb nutrients. These nutrients are then made available to our blood and lymph.

Trees grow in soil teeming with beneficial microorganisms that break down organic matter into nutrients. However, when acid rain falls, it destroys these microorganisms and depletes the soil's nutrients, stunting the tree's growth and weakening its immunity. Toxic metals like aluminum, mercury, arsenic, and cadmium, usually bound to minerals in the soil, are released by the acidic conditions. These metals are then absorbed through the tree's fine root hairs, further poisoning and weakening it.

Over time, the tree's root system breaks down, leading to decay. At this stage, reductive organisms like bacteria, fungi, and mold, which were previously held in check, begin to break down the decaying matter.

So, instead of using pesticides to kill the bugs we deem as an enemy, perhaps we should be asking…

"Why have they arrived on the scene?"

Similarly, our intestines house billions of beneficial microorganisms that help break down food into absorbable nutrients. When acids destroy these beneficial microbes, toxic chemicals and heavy metals clog the villi, inhibiting nutrient absorption. This weakens the body's immunity, especially since a significant portion of our immune system resides in the gut.

At this stage, reductive organisms—bacteria, viruses, fungi, mold, and parasites—appear, breaking down the dead and decaying tissue. They are nature's clean-up crew.

Again, instead of using antibiotics to kill the bugs we deem as an enemy, perhaps we should be asking...

"Why have they arrived on the scene?"

After discussing my *Internal Acid Rain Theory* with my neurologist friend, Dr. Lorne Label, he conducted several pH studies on some of his patients who had been stricken with a neurological disease, such as Parkinson's, Alzheimer's, and multiple sclerosis. We had discussed the latest medical research that revealed Chlamydia bacterium, along with fungus, are almost always present in those suffering from a neurological disease and could be a contributing factor of these devastating conditions.

Agreeing with me that pathogenic microbes are mostly "opportunistic" and are most likely not the originating cause of neurological diseases, he decided to perform several spinal taps on some of his patients to test the pH of their cerebral spinal fluid.

About a month later, Dr. Label reported back...

> *"After contemplating Toni Toney's Internal Acid Rain Theory, I performed spinal taps on some of my Alzheimer's, Parkinson's, and multiple sclerosis patients, as the cerebral spinal fluid is, in effect, the brain's "water" supply and should have the same pH value as blood and lymph—approximately 7.35 – 7.45. ...*
>
> *When I tested the cerebral spinal fluid's pH of these patients, to my amazement, she was right. They all had a pH value of approximately 5.5, the pH of environmental acid rain. Further research is justified to see if shifting the pH of the brain's water supply will provide clues in turning these devastating diseases around. From the evidence I now see, I am optimistic."*

To further validate my *Internal Acid Rain Theory*, Dr. Label and I discussed Louis Pasteur's Germ Theory versus Antoine Béchamp's *Internal Terrain Theory*.

Pasteur's Germ Theory, which posits that diseases are caused by harmful microbes invading from the outside, remains widely accepted. However, Béchamp's Internal Terrain Theory offers a contrasting view: disease arises from within, based on the body's internal environment.

Béchamp discovered microzymas, tiny microorganisms found in all living things, including humans. He proposed that these microzymas existed before all other life forms and that they change form depending on the body's condition. In a toxic, acidic body, microzymas become harmful bacteria and viruses. In a healthy body, they form beneficial microbes.

Béchamp argued that disease is not caused by external germs but by the body's internal environment. Microbes thrive in unhealthy conditions, but they are not the cause of disease—they are simply scavengers. Germs are like flies and maggots that feed on garbage. They appear when the body is in a state of decay, but they do not create that decay.

So again, instead of treating the symptoms with antibiotics, perhaps we should ask…

"How can I clean up my body's toxic mess?"

As the philosopher Pogo once said…

"We have met the real enemy, and the enemy is us!"

The time has come.
The time to FAST with the new moon is now.
The New Earth Fast is how!

– 4 –

THE ANCIENT ART OF FASTING, FORGIVENESS AND PRAYER

Cleanse Out the Old and Shift Into the New

Throughout the years, I have found that the practices of fasting, forgiveness, and prayer—especially when observed during the 7-day new moon phase each month—act like a powerful tsunami, drowning out the voice of the Ego-Mind and allowing the voice of the Spirit-Mind to emerge. It is only then that we can "pass over" into the Promised Land of our hearts—the place where the divine spark of the great I AM THAT I AM invites us to enter. This spark not only frees our souls from the bondage of physical consciousness, but it also creates a dynamic shield around our physical bodies, making us IMMUNE to almost everything!

Fasting not only purges toxic materials and acidic waste from our bodies but also weakens and dismantles the false perception that we are merely physical beings living in a physical world. By fasting on a vibrant array of plant-based foods—especially fruits—during the 7-day new moon phase each month, we can reawaken our seven energy centers of light and reconnect with the true essence of who we are. The new moon phase is the greatest time to shift into the New You!

Forgiveness and prayer are two dynamic forces that have the power to break the bonds of the Ego-Mind—the mind that believes we are separate from God, from nature, and from everything around us—the mind that creates sickness, disease, and death. While forgiveness cleanses our minds of the false beliefs and perceptions that block our true remembrance, the I AM prayer ignites the fiery passion of the great I AM "THAT" I AM within us, bringing into creation the very things we proclaim.

When you make your proclamation to the great, I AM who dwells within you, always choose your words wisely, for when you invoke the name of God—I AM—you are tapping into God's boundless creative power. As you pray for your desires, also imagine that you have already received them. Then, wait patiently, knowing that whatever you have prayed for is already unfolding in the unseen realm of manifestation.

THE ANCIENT ART OF FASTING

To fast means different things to different people. According to the ancients, fasting—whether for religious rites or health purposes—simply meant abstaining from some or all types of food or drink for a specific time and purpose. For spiritual seekers, fasting was a way to open the gateway to the Divine; for those seeking physical healing, it was a method to cleanse the body when unwell.

I've often pondered how and why ancient prophets, such as Moses (c. 1400 BCE) and Daniel (620-538 BCE), fasted. Some believe Moses fasted for 40 days and 40 nights on Mount Sinai to secure answers from God in preparation for a transformational change. In Jewish tradition, the number 40 is associated with the time needed to purify a person in atonement for their "sins." And remember, the word "sin" doesn't mean being a "bad person"—it simply means to forget. When we forget who and what we truly are, we "miss the mark."

The reason for 40 days lies in the natural process of spiritual growth. Just as it takes an embryo 40 days to form in its mother's womb before emerging as a new living being, so too does it take 40 days for a new spiritual being to emerge. Only then can we be ready—like Moses was—to meet the great I AM THAT I AM who dwells within us.

In Christianity, the prophet Daniel is known for receiving visions of an apocalyptic future.

Daniel was chosen by King Nebuchadnezzar, the most powerful of all Babylonian kings, to be a "seer" in his royal court. The king was astonished when Daniel refused to eat at his royal table of meat and wine, believing the king's rich foods would defile him. So, the king allowed Daniel to follow his own diet of pulses for ten days to see if he would become stronger and wiser than the other men at court—and indeed, he did!

It is likely that Daniel followed a raw, plant-based diet—the foods God originally designed for humans to eat before The Fall. In Genesis 1:29, we are told…

> *"I have given you every seed-bearing plant throughout the earth and the fruit trees for your food."*

Plant foods, especially raw fruits from trees, possess the inherent power to not only make us wise and strong, like the prophet Daniel, through their original heirloom seeds (not hybrid, seedless, or GMO), but they inherently possess a dynamic potential to assist us in shifting from The Fall into the Return. The choice is ours!

Modern Fasting Trends
Today, fasting has regained popularity, and a variety of fasting methods have emerged. There are smoothie fasts, juice fasts, fruit fasts, lemonade fasts, herbal fasts, water fasts, dry fasts, and intermittent fasting, the latest trend.

Intermittent fasting involves abstaining from food for specific periods of time and has gained traction among health seekers. Some people practice alternate day fasting, eating normally for 24 hours and fasting on water the next 24 hours. Others may fast for 18-20 hours and eat during a 4 to 6-hour window.

Research is showing that intermittent fasting practices may have the potential to:

- Promote cellular regeneration by triggering autophagy, which is a natural process needed to renew damaged cells.
- Inhibit cancerous growths and chronic disease development.
- Promote normalization of insulin and leptin sensitivity as insulin and leptin resistance are the principal factors for numerous chronic diseases, including diabetes.
- Encourage the body to burn fat for fuel. By limiting your food intake, your body is forced to burn excess body fat, which can

reduce body weight up to 8 percent and decrease body fat up to 16 percent over a period of 3 to 12 weeks.
- Improve cognitive function by providing the brain with fat to burn for energy instead of glucose, which helps in the prevention of Alzheimer's and Parkinson's disease.
- Remove damaged mitochondria, the powerhouse of the cell, and triggers the biogenesis of new mitochondria.

Dr. Herbert Shelton (1861–1952), who supervised the fasts of over 40,000 people during his career, reported numerous case studies where individuals were healed of near-incurable diseases through fasts ranging from a few weeks to 90 days. Dr. Shelton, a lecturer and founder of the Natural Hygiene Society, wrote in his book *Fasting for Renewal of Life*:

Dr. Shelton said…

> *"Healing is a biological process. … It is as much a function of the living organism as respiration, digestion, circulation, excretion, cell proliferation, or nerve activity. It is a ceaseless process, as constant as the turning of the earth on its axis. Man can neither duplicate nor imitate nor provide a substitute for the process. All schools of healing are frauds. … In a fast, the body tears down its defective parts and then builds anew when eating is resumed."*

Dr. Shelton was also the founder of anthroposophy, a movement based on both the natural world as well as the spiritual world, designed for seekers who choose to use natural means to optimize their physical, emotional, and spiritual wellbeing, instead of using unnatural means. He discovered that in a fasting state on nothing but water, the body scours for dead cells, damaged tissues, fatty deposits, tumors, and abscesses, all of which are burned for fuel or expelled as waste.

He testified to both the acuity of mental powers during the fast due to the elimination of such obstructions, as well as restoring the immune system's functionality and cellular metabolism back to their optimum states.

His underlying message was clear...

> *"The freer our bodies are of toxic materials, the clearer our minds are in its ability to think higher, spiritual thoughts."*

Now, there's a new way to fast—the *New Earth Fast*. This method involves a phytochemical-rich smoothie, juice, or fruit fast during the 7-day new moon phase every month. This fast not only cleanses toxic materials from your body, but it also helps prepare your physical body for the shift of the ages—the shift from physical to spiritual consciousness.

Eat Light to Become Light

Most of us have distanced ourselves from nature's table. We've forgotten the true purpose and power of food. Foods grown from seed and soil through the power of photosynthesis, infused with vibrant phytochemicals, are a sacrament—a way to commune with the "light of the world" that dwells within and all around us.

Sadly, most of our educational institutions today teach a limited and myopic view of food, one rooted in a food science theory that measures food based on fats, calories, carbohydrates, and proteins. But from a broader, more anthroposophical perspective, some food scientists are beginning to overturn this outdated viewpoint. They're discovering that plant foods, grown through the power of photosynthesis, are infused with an array of phytochemicals that may redefine food science.

The Power of Photosynthesis

Photosynthesis is the process by which green plants use sunlight, water, and carbon dioxide to create oxygen and energy in the form of complex carbohydrates. The word "photo" in Greek means light, and "synthesis" means to make. In essence, green plants use light energy from the sun to make phytochemicals.

Phytochemicals are compounds found in plants that protect them from environmental threats, such as opportunistic bugs. Research shows that when we consume lots of plant phytochemicals, they may also protect us from such opportunistic threats.

Though scientists have identified thousands of phytochemicals, they're only just beginning to understand the powerful roles these substances play in our health and wellbeing. Debbie Krivitsky, director of clinical nutrition at the Cardiovascular Disease Prevention Center at Harvard-affiliated Massachusetts General Hospital, explains...

> *"We're still learning about phytochemicals, but they may help fight cancer and heart disease."*

The American Institute for Cancer Research now recommends

transitioning to a mostly plant-based diet, as there is growing evidence that phytochemicals—imbued with their rainbow of colors—may have the potential to:

- Aid immune system function
- Protect cells and DNA from damage that may lead to cancer
- Slow the growth rate of some cancer cells
- Reduce inflammation
- Help regulate hormones

In addition to these immune-boosting phytochemicals, plants also produce phytonutrients that nourish, maintain, and restore the health of our cells. Both phytochemicals and phytonutrients are abundant in plant foods such as fruits, vegetables, whole grains, nuts, seeds, and legumes. They come in the seven colors of the rainbow, giving plants their color, flavor, and aroma.

They are the same foods Hippocrates used to heal the sick and the same foods I used to heal myself when, as a young woman, I was hospitalized and near death. They are also the same foods the prophet Daniel consumed to make himself stronger and wiser than any other lad in the king's court.

While I will always remain a student of how to use the "power" of food as medicine to heal the physically sick, I am now also a student of how to use the "purpose" of food as communion—a way to commune with the "light of the world"—a way to heal the spiritually sick.

So, if you're ready to reconnect with your true self, it's time to "Eat

Light" so your physical body's seven sealed energy centers of light can be "turned back on!"

The Electric Universe Theory

I am not a scientist, but as I sat in silence one meditative morning, I began considering the fact that our physical bodies are made up of approximately 100 trillion cells, and each of these cells consists of approximately 100 trillion atoms—all working together to create life.

Most scientists agree that atoms are 99.9999999 percent empty space, but some believe that within this seemingly empty space exists light energy. So, how is it that everything and everyone appears to be physical and tangible to our senses?

While many scientists believe gravity holds everything together, the new science, called the *Electric Universe Theory*, suggests that the true force of attraction in the universe comes from invisible electric currents.

This theory proposes that plasma, the fourth state of matter, permeates space and connects all galaxies in the universe in a vast electrical circuit. Plasma is not only the main component of our Sun but makes up over 99.9 percent of the visible universe.

Interestingly, about 55 percent of our blood is plasma, and the remaining 45 percent are red blood cells, white blood cells and platelets that are suspended in the plasma. Plasma is about 92 percent water.

If this theory is correct, and I believe it is, it could change everything we know about physics and our understanding of the cosmos.

Albert Einstein once said...

> *"Concerning matter, we have been all wrong. What we have called matter is energy whose vibration has been so lowered as to be perceptible to the senses. There is no matter."*

Within this context, doesn't it make sense that if our cells are made up of trillions of atoms, and atoms themselves are composed of light energy, then a diet rich in electrically charged "light energy" foods might hold a power and purpose beyond most scientific understanding?

So, doesn't it stand to reason that the electrical potential found in raw foods could have the ability to prepare our physical bodies for the shift of the ages—the shift that occurs when our seven sealed energy centers of light are "turned back on"?

After all, raw fruits and vegetables, being electrical by nature, align with the electrical properties of our cells.

When we consider that the trillions of cells making up our organs, glands, and tissues are constantly conducting electrical currents to produce energy for nearly every function of the human body, this idea becomes even more plausible. Most scientists agree that even at rest, our bodies can generate around 100 watts of power—enough to light a bulb!

Michael Hickner, an associate professor of materials science and engineering at Penn State, told Live Science that...

> *"Fruits and vegetables conduct electricity in the same way a salt solution will complete an electrical circuit."*

To explore this concept further, I purchased a "fruit clock," a device that runs without a traditional battery. By inserting two probes into raw fruit, the clock runs because fruits and vegetables are high in electrolytes, particularly organic sodium (salt).

However, when the same probes are placed into cooked fruit, the clock doesn't run—because heat destroys the enzyme-mineral component necessary for creating electricity.

This is why I often say...

> *"Let every cell of your body become like an alkaline battery, so you too can keep going on and on!"*

Consider again that our cells are "electrical" due to the movement of charged particles (ions) across their membranes, creating a potential difference (voltage) and enabling electrical signaling.

Now, once again, consider that, just like fish swimming in the waters of our Earth, we have trillions of cells swimming throughout our body's watery terrain. But what happens to fish, or to our cells, when they are forced to swim in toxic waters?

In the 1910s, Dr. Alexis Carrel, a French heart surgeon, biologist, who was awarded the Nobel Prize in Physiology or Medicine, concluded that cells can grow indefinitely; that they are intrinsically immortal.

This claim was based on the tissue culture of a chicken heart that seemed to be able to stay alive forever as long as the tissue's cells remained in a clean, saline (salt) solution environment. This study was conducted in his laboratory at the Rockefeller Institute for Medical Research.

To make sure this happened, Dr. Carrel replaced the saline solution with new fluid that was free of wastes on a daily basis. The reason for this experiment was to understand why we age and why we die. So after 28 years, the purpose of the experiment was achieved, and the experiment ended.

It is reported that Dr. Carrel concluded...

> *"The cell is immortal. It is merely the fluid in which it floats which degenerates. Renew this fluid at intervals, give the cells what they require for nutrition and, as far as we know, the pulsation of life may go on forever!"*

Unfortunately, this experiment has not been replicated since Dr. Carrel's death in 1944, but the results invite us to explore the possibility that cells do not have to age or become cancerous or otherwise diseased.

Clean up the wastes your cells are swimming in, feed them an array of colorful, freshly prepared, phytochemical-nutrient-rich plant foods and, who knows, the possibilities could very well be "endless!"

Fasting expert, Rai Casey, M.D. said...

> *"I had a medical practice for 20 years in NYC, supervised hundreds of long fasts, and I found that the physical healing or weight loss was but a pleasant side effect. What really happened is that the person got in touch with their higher self, their true self, and came to the experience that healing can take place at every level, simply by letting go and allowing Mother Nature to do her work."*

In essence, when we fast every month during the 7-day new moon phase with light energy, electrically charged fruits, the "engine" (mitochondria) within every cell of our physical bodies can amp up the power within our seven sealed energy centers of light so they can once again be turned back on! It is one of the most important things we can do to prepare our physical bodies for the shift of the ages!

So, go ahead—Eat Light—so your physical body's seven seals can open!

Our Physical Body's Seven Energy Centers of Light

As stated in Chapter One, our physical body is the Book of Seven Seals to be opened in the last days. These seals, also known as the seven energy centers of light, are subtle vortexes of energy that spin at unique oscillating rates beyond most of our ability to see them with our physical eyes. Yogic tradition has long called these seven centers, chakras.

Regardless of what they are called, each spiritual center is intricately connected to specific nerve bundles, organs, and glands. Though most of us cannot see them, they interact through two primary systems: the endocrine system and the nervous system.

The Endocrine System

The endocrine system is a network of glands within your body that produce and release hormones that help cells communicate with each other. Hormones act as messengers or chemical signals carried through the bloodstream, regulating and balancing various bodily functions like growth, metabolism, reproduction, and almost everything that occurs within the body.

This system plays a crucial role in the integrative health and wellbeing of the trillions of cells that comprise our organs, glands, and tissues. As mentioned in the Book of Revelation, the seven churches symbolize our body's seven endocrine glands.

These glands release hormones—chemical messengers—that communicate with our nervous system, which in turn shapes our perception of reality. Every thought we think and every feeling we experience either opens or closes our physical body's seven energy centers of light.

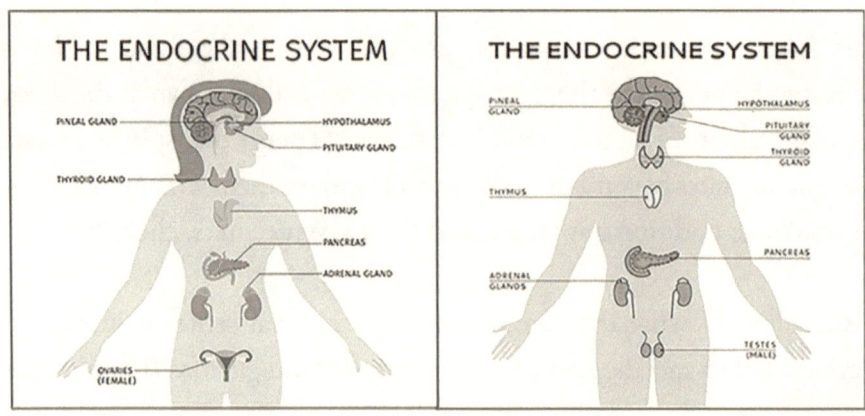

The endocrine system plays a crucial role in:

- Growth and development: Regulating how the body grows and develops.
- Metabolism: Controlling the body's energy production and use.
- Reproduction: Influencing sexual development and function.
- Mood and behavior: Regulating emotions and behaviors.
- Homeostasis: Maintaining a stable internal environment.

The endocrine key glands include:

- Ovaries (in females) and testes (in males): Produce hormones related to sexual development and reproduction.
- Adrenal glands: Produce hormones like adrenaline, which helps the body respond to stress.
- Pancreas: Produces insulin and glucagon, which regulate blood sugar levels.
- Thymus: a vital part of the immune system, primarily responsible for training and maturing T-cells (white blood cells) that help fight infections and diseases.
- Thyroid gland: Produces hormones that control metabolism.
- Pineal gland: regulates sleep-wake cycles and circadian rhythms by secreting the hormone melatonin, which is produced in response to light and darkness.
- Pituitary gland: Often called the "master gland" because it regulates other endocrine glands.

The Nervous System

The nervous system is a complex network of nerves and cells that controls your body's actions and responses. It's made up of the brain, spinal cord, and nerves. Its primary function is to coordinate and control all bodily activities by transmitting signals (electrical and chemical) between the brain, spinal cord, and the rest of the body. This enables us to think, feel, move, and react to the environment.

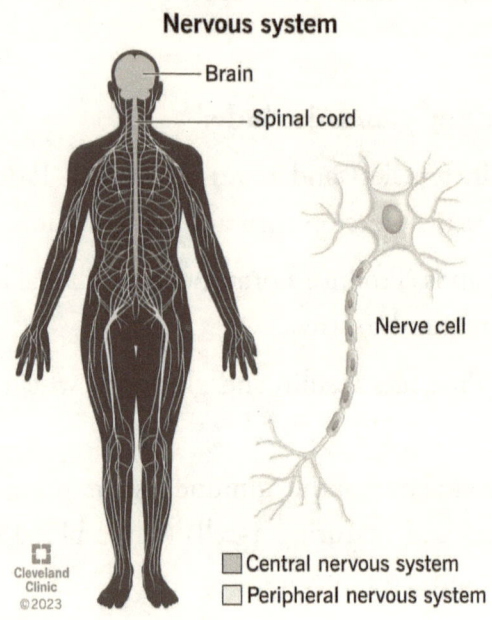

This is how the nervous system works:

- The nervous system sends electrical signals between the brain and the rest of the body.
- The brain and spinal cord receive and process sensory information from your senses.

- The nervous system responds to this information by triggering reactions, such as making your muscles move or causing you to feel pain.

What does the nervous system control?
- Thoughts and memory: The nervous system regulates complicated processes like thoughts and memory.
- Movement: The nervous system controls voluntary movements, like walking and speaking, as well as involuntary movements, like breathing and blinking.
- Sensation: The nervous system controls sight, hearing, taste, smell, and feeling.
- Stress: The nervous system controls how the body reacts in stressful situations.

The endocrine system works in tandem with the nervous system to detect and transmit signals from both internal and external stimuli, helping to maintain homeostasis. Together, these two systems regulate the electrical and chemical processes that relay information between the brain and the body, ensuring smooth communication and balance.

Again, they play a significant role in opening or veiling out physical body's seven energy centers of light.

Our Physical Body's Book of Seven Seals
The "Book of Seven Seals" contained within our physical body, to be opened in the "last days," refers to our seven spiritual centers of light, which extend from the base of the spine to just above the top of the head.

The lower three centers connect us to the visible physical world; the upper three centers connect us to the invisible spiritual world; and the fourth center is the bridge between them—the center that connects the physical with the spiritual.

The color of the first energy center is red. Its element is AIR.

The endocrine glands associated with this center are the gonads— ovaries or testicles. Its collaborating organs include the kidneys and bladder. It is the center of sexuality, fluidity, and fertility. It governs your emotions, creativity, sensitivity, intimacy, and self-expression.

This center is about feeling emotionally secure with yourself. When it is open, you will feel sensuous, open to pleasure, creative, fluid, and receptive to shifting changes like the ocean's tides. If it is clogged with toxic thoughts, beliefs and perceptions, you may feel sexual guilt and shame and feel undeserving of a pleasurable, abundant, creative life.

Some red foods that have the phytochemical power to ramp up this energy center's light are:

Strawberries	Red cherries	Red apples	Watermelon
Raspberries	Red grapes	Red beets	Pomegranates
Pink grapefruit	Plums	Red pears	Cranberries
Red peppers	Red cabbage	Chili peppers	Radish
Tomatoes	Red onion	Red potatoes	Radicchio

The color of the second energy center is orange. Its element is FIRE.

The endocrine gland associated with this center is the adrenals. Its collaborating organ is the appendix. It is the center of physical energy, grounding, and self-preservation. It governs the back, feet, hips, spine, and legs.

This center is about us feeling at home wherever we are. When it is open, you will feel supported, grounded with the earth, and safe in the world you live in… no matter what may be happening in the world around you. However, if this center is clogged with toxic thoughts, beliefs, and perceptions, you may feel fearful, unstable, and unsure.

Some orange foods that have the phytochemical power to ramp up this energy center's light are:

Oranges	Apricots	Cantaloupe	Mangoes
Papaya	Nectarines	Tangerines	Peaches
Passion fruit	Persimmons	Carrots	Acorn squash
Yams	Pumpkin	Orange peppers	Sweet potatoes

The color of the third energy center is yellow. Its element is EARTH.

The endocrine glands associated with this center are the pancreas and liver (glandular organs). Its collaborating organs include the spleen, stomach, intestines, gallbladder and colon. It is the center of your body's most dynamic energy powerhouse. It governs your self-esteem, sense of purpose, personal identity, individual will, digestion and metabolism.

When it is open, your energy will be strong and flow like a mighty river, making you feel empowered, aligned with your sense of purpose, and ready to be the change you want to see in the world! But if it is clogged with toxic thoughts, false beliefs and perceptions, you may feel a sense of powerlessness, low self-esteem, or no real sense of purpose. You may be constipated and quick to anger.

Some yellow foods that have the phytochemical power to ramp up this energy center's light are:

Bananas	Pineapples	Lemons
Yellow kiwi	Yellow pears	Yellow apples
Yellow figs	Grapefruit	Corn
Squash	Yellow peppers	Yukon Gold potatoes

The color of the fourth energy center is green. Its element is WATER.

The endocrine gland associated with this center is the thymus. Its collaborating organs include the lungs and heart. It is the center of love for oneself and others, compassion, empathy and forgiveness. It governs unconditional love, service to others, and your complete faith in Spirit.

It is also the gateway between Heaven and Earth; the bridge that integrates the physical reality with the spiritual reality and beyond. When it is open, you will feel a sense of selflessness, immense joy, compassion, bliss, unconditional love for everything and everyone, and knowing that love is truly who and what you truly are! If this center is clogged with toxic thoughts, beliefs and perceptions, you may feel a sense of loneliness, disappointment, grief, and a longing for love that never gets fulfilled.

Some green foods that have the phytochemical power to ramp up this energy center's light are:

Green grapes	Green apples	Green pears
Green kiwi	Lime	Honeydew melon
Avocado	Cucumbers	Celery
Asparagus	Artichokes	Arugula
Spirulina	Broccoli	Lettuce
Kale	Zucchini	Green beans
Spinach	Collards	Brussels Sprouts
Green peppers	Cabbage	Spirulina

The color of the fifth energy center is blue. Its element is ETHER.

The endocrine gland associated with this center is the thyroid. It's collaborating organ is the respiratory system. It is the center of communication, speech and hearing. It governs clear, effective and conscious communication with yourself, others, and with Spirit.

When this center is open, you will be able to speak your truth with yourself and others with utmost authenticity, be a better listener, and be able to commune with Spirit in ways you thought were impossible. On the other hand, if this center is clogged with toxic thoughts, beliefs and perceptions, you may feel like you're unable to express yourself properly, unable to find your voice, or speak your truth. You may also be overly talkative, not a good listener or be unable to care about what others have to say.

The color of the sixth energy center is indigo. Its element is LIGHT.

The endocrine gland associated with this center is the pineal gland. Its collaborating organs include the eyes, nose, face and brain. It is the center of illumination, higher knowledge, intuition or what some call, your sixth sense. It governs wisdom, visualization, fantasy, determination, self-initiation, and the understanding of your purpose in life.

When this center is open, your eyes will become single and your whole body will become filled with light! If it is clogged with toxic thoughts, beliefs, and perceptions, you may feel closed minded, too attached to logic, untrusting and cynical.

The color of the seventh energy center is violet. Its element is STARDUST.

The endocrine gland associated with this center is the pituitary gland. Its collaborating organ is the brain. It is the center of enlightenment and ascension. It governs faith, spiritual connection, higher consciousness, infinite energy, and transformation.

I believe that this center is the "seat of the soul;" the place where the veil of amnesia is lifted. When it is open, you will be raptured into a deep sense of your oneness with God, nature, and everything and everyone around you. If this center is clogged with toxic thoughts, beliefs and perceptions, you may feel a sense of separation; ultimately leading to a lack of faith, confusion, inability to trust, and being overly concerned with what's happening outside of you.

Some blue, indigo, and violet foods that have the phytochemical power to ramp up these three energy centers' lights are:

Black cherries	Blueberries	Blackberries
Figs	Concord grapes	Purple grapes
Elderberries	Plums	Black currants
Passion fruit	Mulberries	Prunes
Eggplant	Purple cabbage	Black radish

In conclusion, what today's research has discovered is that when we consume an array of colorful, phytochemical-nutrient-rich foods every day that, just like they can protect plants from environmental threats, they may also can protect us from plague-like viruses, bacterial and parasitical infections. The more we consume, the greater our protection.

That's why I say...

A color-a-day keeps plagues away!

FEAST while you FAST

Cleansing your body with an array of colorful light energy, electrically charged fruits for seven days during the new moon phase will help you prepare your physical body for the shift of the ages. This quantum shift is the shift from The Fall—the fallen state of consciousness where you have forgotten who and what you truly are, and the shift into The Return—the risen state of consciousness where we remember who and what we truly are. While this journey is not an easy task, it is one we must all take when we are ready to shift from the old and into the new.

The 7-Day New Moon Fruit Fast

Sadly, there are those who believe that we should avoid fruit like the plague! They say that fruits are bad for us; that they are loaded with sugar. But isn't it interesting that sugar is the by-product of photosynthesis? So to all of you fruit-sugar-avoiders out there, think again.

The sugar in the fruits we eat is not the problem! The problem is the body's inability to convert that sugar into pure energy! The question then becomes... why can't it?

One of the primary reasons is because most people have been eating the "wrong types of fat" for way too long.

The human body was never designed to consume fats from concentrated oils that have been extracted from whole plants, especially seed oils such as canola, soy, or sunflower. These unnatural types of fats are difficult to digest and assimilate.

When a person has consumed these types of difficult to digest and assimilate fats over their lifetime, they begin to accumulate around the "skin" (membrane) of our cells, which creates a type of filmy, lipid coating. Then, when the pancreas secretes insulin to be carried into the cell so it can be converted into pure energy, the insulin is unable to penetrate the lipid coating, so it builds up in the blood stream.

This then creates everything from insulin resistance to type-2 diabetes, to candida, to fungal infections, and possibly even cancer. (For more information, read Oncologist, Dr. Simoncini's book, *Cancer is a Fungus!*)

Ecologically speaking, it's like what happens whenever an oil spill occurs in the waterways of our planet. If the spilled oil is left to accumulate on the "skin" of the fish, the fish will be unable to breathe, so they die!

A similar ecological breakdown happens to the trillions of cells that swim throughout our body's waterways when we consume the wrong types of fats!

Therefore, fruits are not the problem—the wrong types of fats are! Not only was our body designed to eat fruit, but it was also designed to thrive on it!

The 7-Day New Moon Smoothie Fast
The health benefits of drinking an array of colorful, freshly prepared, photochemical-nutrient-rich organic smoothies for seven days during the new moon phase are enormous. They have been shown to help with excess weight gain, hydration, unhealthy food cravings, better digestion, building a strong immunity, detoxification, skin disorders, depression, bone health, heart disorders, mood swings, and hormonal dysfunction... just to name a few.

If you're a beginner or intermediate faster, when fasting for seven days during new moon phase, I recommend either eating lots of fruit or drinking lots of smoothies every day as the fiber in both is known to absorb toxins, which helps to slow down the detoxification process.

Also, for those who live a fast-paced lifestyle, smoothies are easier to prepare and a less wasteful way to fast than juicing as you'll be utilizing the whole plant. In essence, you'll be blending the seeds, pits, stems, pith, and other plant parts into your favorite smoothie recipe, which offers even more phytochemical-nutrient health benefits.

So, when blending up a smoothie, consider that you'll be blending then drinking the corresponding chakra color of each plant food you have chosen to add to your smoothie; thus, filling your body's seven spiritual centers with the light energy of the sun!

The 7-Day New Moon Juice Fast

Fasting on an array of colorful, freshly prepared photochemical-nutrient-rich organic juices during the 7-day new moon phase is like receiving a "blood transfusion" from nature! In essence, the juice of a plant is the "blood of a plant!" And while most people have never thought about plant blood... the truth is, plants have blood, just like us!

What's truly amazing is that plant blood looks similar to human blood under a high-powered microscope. The major difference is that plant blood carries a magnesium molecule whereas human blood contains an iron molecule. The other difference is the color—magnesium is what makes plant blood green, and iron is what makes human blood red.

In essence, while blending pulverizes the whole edible part of fruits and vegetables, juicing just extracts the blood of the plant. Because the fiber has been removed, there's virtually no need to digest anything, so all the enzymes, vitamins, minerals, sugars, and proteins are quickly absorbed and metabolized. Thus, juicing gives your digestive system time to rest, regenerate and recharge, while also taking in an array of colorful, phytochemical-nutrients.

Drinking lots of freshly prepared organic juices, imbued with various colors every day, has the power to expunge mucus and eradicate acids and toxins from every part of the body. The great news is that a juice fast, especially during the 7-day new moon phase every month, will not only assist your body in eliminating toxic, acidic build-up, it will also assist in preparing your body for the shift of the ages.

So, during the 7-day new moon phase every month, you'll be juicing and drinking the colors of various plants that correspond with the seven light energy centers of your body: red, orange, yellow, green, blue, indigo, and violet—thus, filling your body's seven spiritual centers with the light energy of the sun.

So, go ahead—Enlighten Yourself—so your physical body's seven seals can open!

THE FORGIVENESS FAST

The 7-Day New Moon Forgiveness Fast, paired with the I AM prayer outlined below, forms a deeply powerful process for releasing limiting beliefs and false perceptions. This transformative practice offers a path to letting go of memories and patterns that no longer serve you. In essence, the forgiveness fast is about shedding the constraints of physical consciousness, allowing you to elevate into a higher, ascended state of spiritual awareness.

While the forgiveness fast focuses on releasing the old—whether it's limiting beliefs, grudges, or negative perceptions that keep you tethered to the past—prayer is about embracing the new. It affirms the positive, hopeful, and abundant possibilities you wish to manifest in your life. Together, these practices form an incredibly potent combination, particularly when undertaken during the new moon, a time of renewal and fresh beginnings.

The Forgiveness Fast: Ho'oponopono

The most transformative forgiveness practice I've personally experienced is the ancient Hawaiian tradition of ho'oponopono, which translates to "to make right." This process offers a powerful way to release negative emotions or perceptions that prevent us from living as our highest and best selves. It also emphasizes the importance of collective consciousness, reminding us that we are all interconnected in this great circle of life.

In the ho'oponopono tradition, forgiveness isn't limited to others—it also involves forgiving ourselves and the perceptions that may have caused us pain. Forgiveness is not just an individual act; it's a collective one. When one person suffers, the entire group is considered affected. By cleansing our consciousness, we contribute to healing not only yourself but also the entire group or community.

The process involves four simple but powerful phrases:
- (1) I love you.
- (2) I'm sorry.
- (3) Please forgive me.
- (4) Thank you.

These four phrases facilitate self-forgiveness, release negative emotions, and promote healing by acknowledging wrongdoing and fostering self-love and gratitude.

"I love you!"
This phrase signifies self-love and acceptance, as well as love for the Divine and compassion for others. It's a reminder to treat yourself and others with kindness and understanding.

"I'm sorry!"

This phrase acknowledges responsibility for any negative thoughts, actions, or emotions that may have contributed to disharmony or conflict within yourself and others. It's a step towards taking ownership of our part in a situation, even if you don't feel personally responsible.

"Please forgive me!"

This phrase is not about "letting someone off the hook"; it's a request for shifting our perspectives—both for ourselves and others—for any perceived or actual wrongs. It's a way of cleansing the burden of guilt for something you may have done in the past, which makes space for a new perspective to emerge. Guilt always demands punishment, so let's cleanse the old which allows our innocence to come forward. This is what it means, to be born again!

"Thank you!"

This phrase expresses gratitude for the opportunity to learn and grow, even through a challenging experience. It acknowledges the value of the situation and fosters a sense of peace and contentment.

These four phrases are said to carry the same frequency as that created by monks during meditation. The results from this practice are truly remarkable. It's simple: you don't ask for forgiveness to get something or change anything. The sole purpose of forgiveness is to cleanse yourself of limiting beliefs and false perceptions. It's like taking a consciousness shower. Just as showering cleans us but must be done daily to keep us clean, the same is true for forgiveness. We practice ho'oponopono daily to become—and stay—clean.

The Transformative Power of Ho'oponopono
The effectiveness of this forgiveness process was powerfully demonstrated in a remarkable story shared by Joe Vitale in his book Zero Limits. Dr. Stanley Hew Len, a clinical psychologist, used ho'oponopono to heal an entire ward of criminally insane patients at the Hawaiian State Hospital. Dr. Len never met the patients in person; instead, he reviewed their charts and focused on cleansing his own consciousness of any belief in mental illness. Miraculously, many of the patients healed.

This story raises an intriguing question:

- What if the world we see around us is simply a reflection of our inner consciousness?
- What if the suffering we perceive "outside" of ourselves is merely a projection of false beliefs or perceptions we hold within ourselves, like a mirror?

Changing the Perception of Separation
The concept that "there's only one of us here" is central to ho'oponopono. It challenges the belief in separation—whether between ourselves and others, the physical and the spiritual, or the various aspects of what we perceive as reality. The goal is to dismantle the illusion of separation, as this belief is the root cause of discord, sickness, and suffering in our world.

Practical Applications of Ho'oponopono
Again, the ho'oponopono fogiveness process is about connecting with the Divine and the Divine within whoever or whatever you are forgiving—always remembering—there's only one of us here!.

(1) If someone you care for is sick, repeat to yourself or out loud as you visualize this person in your mind:

- I love you.
- I'm sorry for believing that sickness is even possible.
- Please forgive me for using my consciousness in such an unwise way.
- Thank you for restoring my consciousness to a state of perfect health.

(2) If you're witnessing chaos in the world, repeat:

- I love you.
- I'm sorry for believing that [insert chaos] is even possible.
- Please forgive me for using my consciousness in such an unwise way.
- Thank you for undoing this belief and restoring my mind to a state of peace and harmony for all.

(3) If you're holding anger or resentment, repeat:

- I love you.
- I'm sorry for the anger and resentment that I've held in my heart for [name of the person or situation].
- Please forgive me for using my consciousness in such an unwise way.
- Thank you for cleansing and restoring my consciousness to LOVE.

For self-healing, the moment you wake up in the morning, instead of turning on the news or checking your emails, consider keeping your eyes closed, connecting with your breath, left hand over your heart, right hand over your belly and repeat to yourself...

"I love you!" (connect to the power of the great I AM within you).
"I'm sorry!" (for believing that disease is even possible).
"Please forgive me!" (for using my consciousness in this unwise way).
"Thank you!" (for restoring my consciousness to perfect health).

Alternatively, you can simply repeat the four phrases like a mantra, over and over, with the awareness that you've identified where you've been holding a similar destructive thought or negative attitude. Take a moment, close your eyes, go inward to that quiet place, and silently repeat these four phrases. You can say them to yourself, to the Divine, or even to another.

The Role of Our Thoughts
Our thoughts shape our reality. They form our beliefs, which in turn shape our perceptions, and ultimately, create the realities we experience. The work of forgiveness and cleansing through ho'oponopono is an opportunity to reset these patterns and beliefs. If we truly believe in our interconnectedness and the collective consciousness, we can begin to see that healing ourselves also heals the world around us.

Internationally renowned Japanese scientist Masaru Emoto, in his book *The Hidden Messages in Water*, demonstrated how our thoughts, words, and emotions profoundly influence water molecules— either positively or negatively. In his studies, Emoto found that water exposed to positive words and intentions formed beautiful, symmetrical crystalline structures when frozen, while water exposed to negative words and intentions formed disorganized, asymmetrical structures.

Along with cleansing the body of toxic waste, consider the type of thoughts, words, and feelings you are sending into the waters of your body? Be aware that the messages you send shape your reality and, ultimately, your life.

As I reflected on the messages I had been sending to the waters of my body, I concluded...

> *Wherever your focus of attention goes, your chemistry flows. Likewise, wherever your focus of attention goes, your reality flows. Shift your focus of attention on that which you want instead of what you don't want and watch, as the world within and all around you shifts! You have nothing to do but this!*

This was a profound prophetic awakening!

As Morrnah Nalamaku Simeona, a renowned Kahuna and healer, said...

> *"If we can accept that we are the sum total of all past thoughts, emotions, words, deeds, and actions, then we can begin to see how a process of correcting or setting aright can change our lives, our families, and our society."*

The Collective Shift

The idea that a small group of people can shift the collective consciousness is rooted in many traditions. Some believe that 144,000 people are enough to create a profound shift in consciousness and bring about positive change. This concept aligns with the teachings of quantum physicist Max Planck, who recognized that our perception shapes our reality.

Max Planck said...

> *"When you change the way you look at things, the things you look at change."*

This quote strikes at the heart of human experience, suggesting that our perception has the power to shape our reality. It serves as a philosophical gem, reminding us of the immense power of perspective, thus how we see things.

By focusing on health, peace, and love, we can shift our consciousness and, in turn, shift the collective consciousness of our world. When enough of us clean our minds and align with love for ourselves and each other, the world will reflect that change.

One morning, as I was practicing ho'oponopono, I had a personal experience of its transformational power. As a small child, I was taught in church that Eve, the first woman, was the cause of the "Fall" of man, and as a result, all subsequent women were deemed guilty. I recalled the sensation of a noose tightening around my small neck, choking off the power of my feminine existence. Interestingly, I had suffered from neck pain for much of my life. Guilt was my noose, and the realization of my innocence was my release.

Conclusion: Be the Change

The Forgiveness Fast is an invitation to clean our consciousness, forgive ourselves and others, and embrace the love that is inherent in all things. By practicing ho'oponopono every day, not just during the 7-day new moon phase, we align with the wisdom of ancient traditions and contribute to the healing of both our individual self and the collective consciousness.

So, why not cleanse out the old so you can shift into the new consciousness, a perception that creates a healthier, loving, peaceful, and thriving world?

As Mahatma Gandhi said…

> *"Be the change you want to see in the world"*

The 7-DAY NEW MOON I AM Prayer

The 7-Day New Moon I AM Prayer is an ancient practice that transcends the conventional view of prayer as a request for help. It represents a deeper, more transformative connection with the Divine.

The roots of this practice can be traced back to the Bible, where Moses, upon encountering the Great Light on Mount Sinai, asked, "Who are you?"

The Great Light replied, "I AM THAT I AM."

This phrase is profound because it signifies our inner connection with the Divine as co-creators to become whatever we affirm it to be.

The I AM prayer follows the structure: "I AM _____ THAT which I desire—I AM."

For example: "I AM financially wealthy—I AM!"

The final "I AM" is your declaration and faith that it is DONE!

At its core, the I AM prayer is a powerful affirmation, asserting that our words carry creative power and can manifest positive outcomes.

While traditional prayers in many religious practices are viewed as pleas to a distant God for help, the I AM practice shifts this perspective. It's not about begging for assistance from an outside source; rather, it's about declaring, affirming, and aligning with the very essence of who we are in relationship to the creative power of God within us. It invites us to recognize the profound oneness between ourselves and the Divine.

The Creative Power of I AM

As previously mentioned, the words "I AM" are considered the most powerful words we can speak. This is because "I AM" is the name of God, of Christ, of the Divine that dwells within us—the name of CREATION itself!

Whatever follows the words "I AM" is what shapes your reality. In essence, when you say, "I AM," you are invoking the creative power of the Divine within you, setting the intention to manifest whatever comes after those words… I AM THAT!

The second "I AM" in the phrase represents the answered prayer, as though the desired outcome has already been realized. In the spiritual realm, time is irrelevant—everything exists in the Now. This is the transformative power of the I AM prayer: it connects you to the present moment and the limitless possibilities of manifestation.

When you speak these words, you are not just saying something out loud—you are aligning with the infinite possibilities that are already present within you. The question is: What are you attaching to your "I AM"? So, before you speak another word, keep in mind that your words shape your reality, so it's essential to be mindful of the words you use.

What Are You Creating with Your Words?
Consider the common statements that many people unconsciously attach to "I AM:"

I AM sick.	I AM broke.
I AM tired.	I AM afraid.
I AM weak	I AM frustrated.
I AM ugly.	I AM worried.
I AM fat.	I AM guilty.

Each of these declarations becomes a self-fulfilling prophecy. Your focus and words shape your experience. Wherever your attention goes, your reality flows.

Shift Your Focus
Instead of focusing on what you don't want, the I AM prayer invites you to shift your attention to what you do want. Begin using the I AM affirmation with positive, constructive, and life-affirming words.

I AM healthy.	I AM beautiful
I AM full of energy.	I AM slim.
I AM strong.	I AM content.
I AM wealthy.	I AM peaceful.
I AM confident.	I AM innocent.

Always remember that the words you speak after the name of God—I AM—are shaping your future. These affirmations are not mere wishes; they are powerful declarations of whatever you wish to manifest in your life. The more consistently you speak these words with conviction, using the creative power of your imagination as if they have already come to pass, the more they will shape your reality.

The I AM Prayer and Visualization

To make the I AM prayer even more powerful, use your imagination to visualize your desired outcome. Visualization is a potent tool for reshaping your reality, as it allows you to mentally and emotionally align with the life you wish to create. When you combine visualization with the I AM prayer, you amplify the creative power within you.

Albert Einstein famously said…

> *"Imagination is everything. It is the preview of life's coming attractions."*

So, let's imagine together:

- A world where sickness and disease do not exist.
- A world where health and prosperity are the norm.
- A life of knowing that the great I AM within us knows how to heal everything.
- A world where peace abounds, and people love each other as themselves.

This is the future—together, we have the power to create the "New Earth." It is a consciousness that brings forth the "New You" in a world that has been lost for thousands of years.

The Time to Act is Now!

The *New Earth Fast*, combined with Forgiveness and Prayer, is a call to action. The time to fast, forgive, and pray during the 7-day new moon phase is now. These practices help cleanse and align your body, mind, and spirit with the highest version of yourself. They serve as a powerful reminder that you are a master, capable of shaping your reality by shifting your beliefs, perceptions, and actions.

Now is the time to create the life you desire and become the highest, best version of yourself.

Through fasting, forgiveness, and the transformative power of the I AM prayer, you have the power to unlock your full potential and manifest the life you've always dreamed of—for yourself, your planet, and others.

The practice of the I AM prayer reminds you that you are one with God, one with nature, and one with everything and everyone around you. Always remember, you are deeply connected to the Divine. Through the power of your words and consciousness, you have the ability to create the New Earth.

In conclusion, by practicing the I AM prayer, you are not merely praying for change—you are becoming the change! Fasting, forgiveness, and prayer during the 7-day new moon phase is the path toward true freedom, fulfillment, and empowerment.

The time has come.
The time to FAST, FORGIVE and PRAY is now.
The New Earth Fast is how!

PART TWO
The Fast

NEW EARTH FAST

– 5 –

THE NEW EARTH FAST
Cleanse to Enlighten Yourself

So, if it's the new moon and you're ready to create the new you, let's get started. The items needed for your *New Earth Fast* include 1 2-ounce bottle of organic lobelia tincture, 1 1-ounce bottle of organic cayenne tincture, 1 bottle of your favorite "gut flush" formula, 1 bag "Makai" Celtic Sea Salt®, 1 bag of Celtic bath salts, a dry skin brush, and a roll of pH paper or packet of strips. Most of these items can be found at your favorite health food store, on line, or on my personal website: tonitoney.com.

Shopping List
1 2-ounce bottle lobelia tincture
1 1-ounce bottle cayenne tincture
1 bottle of your favorite "gut flush" formula
1 bag "Makai" Celtic Sea Salt®
1 bag Celtic bath salts
1 dry skin brush
1 roll of pH paper or packet of strips

Check Your Saliva pH

Before beginning the fast, it's always a good idea to check your first morning saliva pH. Because our bodies are made up of approximately 75 percent water, and water is made up of 90 percent oxygen, this measurement is one of the most important ways to help determine the state of your overall health.

While there are many tests you can take to determine the state of your overall health, I have concluded that the first morning saliva pH test is one of the simplest, easiest, in-home tests you can do. It's a test that I call an *Internal Acid-Rain Study* that you can take as an indicator of the health of your "inner seas." After all, the human body is a living ecosystem, so why not consider taking the complexity of what we call disease and consider looking at it through a different lens?

The acronym pH stands for potential of hydrogen. It's used to describe the acidity or alkalinity of fluids. The pH scale ranges from 0 to 14. The readings are based around a neutral pH of 7:

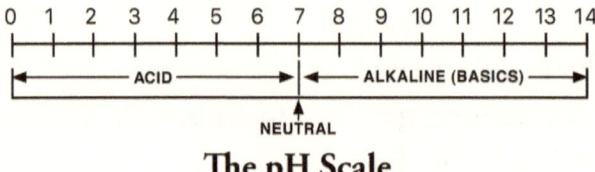

The pH Scale

A pH slightly below 7 is acidic and oxygen levels become depleted in an acidic state.

A pH slightly higher than 7 is alkaline and oxygen levels are sustained in an alkaline state.

The "inner seas" of the human body are designed to be slightly alkaline. When a person is healthy, the pH of their saliva typically ranges between 7.2 and 7.4. In simpler terms, when your pH levels fall within this range, your blood oxygen levels are likely also optimal. This means that the cells in your body, swimming in these "inner seas," are thriving because harmful microorganisms (such as viruses, bacteria, candida, and fungi) thrive in more acidic (low-oxygen) environments. On the other hand, when your pH levels drop below this range, your blood oxygen levels tend to decrease as well, potentially affecting cellular health.

The easiest way to test the pH of your body's "inner seas" is by measuring the pH of your first morning saliva. To do this, use a strip of pH paper before drinking water or brushing your teeth.

Saliva pH Test Made Easy

1. Upon awakening, fill your mouth with saliva, stir with your tongue, and then swallow. Do this several times to help ensure that your saliva is clean.
2. Fill your mouth with saliva then put some clean saliva onto a small strip of pH paper.
3. Wait 20 seconds and compare the resulting color to the pH strip's color chart.

Saliva pH Results Made Easy

1. If your first morning saliva pH is between 7.2 and 7.4, the "inner seas" your cells are swimming in are in a healthy, ecologically balanced pH range.
2. If your saliva pH is between 7.0 and 6.5, you are slightly acidic.

3. If your saliva pH is between 6.5 and 5.5, you are mildly acidic.
4. If your saliva pH is between 5.5 and 4.5, you are severely acidic.

In summary, the lower your measurement is on the pH scale, the more acidic your "inner seas" are, and the more deficient you are in cellular oxygen and alkaline minerals; the greater the acidity, the greater the depletion. Research shows that virtually every degenerative disease, including cancer, heart disease, osteoporosis, arthritis, and even tooth decay, are often associated with excess acidity.

This why I have long said that the most important key to maintaining or regaining your overall health is to *Alkalize Yourself!*

Determine Your Fasting Level

If your saliva pH is moderately or severely acidic and you begin cleansing too quickly, you might experience what health practitioners call a healing crisis. This can include symptoms like dizziness, headaches, fatigue, or even more severe reactions. If this happens to you, be gentle with yourself—start your fasting regimen gradually. You may want to begin with a three-day fast instead of a full seven days, or perhaps try a combination of both. Eating fruit or drinking smoothies can be a good option.

Fiber helps absorb toxins and can buffer the effects of cleansing, so be mindful of your fasting choices. The more acidic your pH, the slower you should approach your fast.

Additionally, don't be alarmed if your saliva pH becomes more acidic during a 7-day fast. This could be a sign that your body is releasing long-held, acidic toxins. For this reason, it's best to avoid measuring your pH again until after the fast is completed.

The following are my fasting level recommendations:
- If your pH level is 6.0 or under: Fruit Fast.
- If your pH level is between 6.0 and 6.5: Smoothie Fast.
- If your pH level is between 6.5 and 7.4: Juice Fast.

Begin your fast by gathering a variety of colorful organically-grown fruits and vegetables. Choose your favorite, seasonal, ripe reds, oranges, yellows, greens, blues, violets, and indigo fruits and vegetables from your garden, local farmer's market, or health-food store.

Then...

Eat them up! Blend them up! Or...Juice them up!

Enlighten Me
7 Colors for 7 Days

Fruit Fast

Eating just fruit for seven days each month isn't only simple—it's truly transformational. Fruits were the original foods of Eden! Moreover, fruits are the absolute BEST antioxidant "fast foods" ever, provided to us by nature! For seven short days each month, all you need to do to cleanse your body of the unnatural toxic waste that causes you to feel fat, sick, and tired is to "pick and peel." That means selecting the ripest, seasonally grown fruits available, peeling them (if necessary), and eating them!

For even more powerful cleansing results, consider trying a mono-fruit fast. This means you'll eat only one type of fruit of the same color each day for seven days.

For example:

> **Day One:** Red only
>
> **Day Two:** Orange only
>
> **Day Three:** Yellow only
>
> **Day Four:** Green only
>
> **Day Five:** Blue only
>
> **Day Six:** Indigo only
>
> **Day Seven:** Violet only

This way, you'll be giving your digestive system a much-needed rest while flushing accumulated toxins and wastes out of the tissues of your body.

Enlighten Me
7 Colors for 7 Days

Smoothie Fast

Blended fruit and vegetable drinks, commonly known as smoothies, are gentle cleansers for the body. Not only are they easy to make, but they are also delicious. Best of all, they'll keep you from feeling hungry during your fast, as they are packed with fiber. Unlike a juice fast, you won't experience that persistent hunger sensation, making it more likely that you'll be able to complete the full seven days.

A smoothie fast is also perfect for those with an on-the-go lifestyle. Simply pour your blended smoothie into a to-go bottle and take it with you. Alternatively, you can pack a bag of fruit and a portable blender to make a fresh blend wherever you are, whenever you want. Sipping on a smoothie throughout the day will also help keep your energy levels high.

1. Choose a blender that's up for a high-fiber "blend light" smoothie fast task. The blenders I recommend are among the best of the best high-speed workhorses. If you're on a budget, the NutriBullet Rx with 1500 horse power is relatively inexpensive. On the higher dollar end are BlendTec and VitaMix blender. With any of these blenders, your blending task will be made easy!

2. Choose the base liquid you would like to use. I use freshly prepared fruit juices such orange, apple and grape or veggie juices such as celery, carrot and beet, depending on the "color of the day!"

Sometimes I use plain ole' water or coconut water. Be as creative and mindful as you can while preparing the smoothie that smells and tastes like manna from heaven!

3. Choose your favorite smoothie recipes or be creative and create your own. Even though I'm offering my favorite smoothie recipes, feel free to deviate from them and make up your own recipes. Simply keep in mind that organization is a huge factor in your *New Earth Fast* success.

Be sure to purchase (or grow your own!) organic produce. Fresh is always best. However, if fresh isn't available, feel free to use frozen organic fruits such as berries, mango, and pineapple grown in the "good ole'" USA by Cascadian Farms.

The typical smoothie recipe is full of vitamins, antioxidants, fiber, protein, and other phytochemical-nutrients, giving your body what it needs for a gentle phytochemical-nutrient-rich cleansing flush. They also contains a large amount of water, which helps to hydrate your body, while boosting your metabolism.

Enlighten Me Smoothie Recipes

During a smoothie fast, you'll be using just one recipe each day, so feel free to make as much as you want! Some health-conscious individuals like to add fats, such as avocado, nuts, or seeds, to their fruit smoothies. In my opinion, that's a big no-no! The reason? Fruits and fats don't mix!

Make sure to scrub, trim, destem, peel, and slice all your fruits and veggies as needed. Always wash unpeeled fruit before you peel it, as bacteria and other contaminants on the skin can enter the fruit as you cut it. Keep in mind that many fruit or veggie skins, seeds, and stems can also be blended in for a more wholesome and nutrient-rich smoothie.

For those of you who've never made a smoothie before, don't worry—it's really fun and as easy as 1-2-3!

> Step One: Add all ingredients to blender.
> Step Two: Blend until smooth.
> Step Three: Enjoy!

– Enlighten Me Acai –

2 cups water
1 cup red raspberries
1 orange, peeled
1 banana, peeled
2 green apples, cored
1 packet frozen acai berries
BLEND.

– Enlighten Me Berries –

2 cups water
1 cup strawberries
3-4 Valencia oranges, peeled
1 cup yellow kiwi
1 cup green grapes
1 cup blueberries
BLEND.

Note: The green, leafy strawberry stems can be included in your smoothie, if they are fresh. When peeling oranges, leave plenty of white pith for blending.

– Enlighten Me Tropics –

1 cup coconut water
1 small red papaya, deseeded, peeled, chunked
1 large mango, peeled and pitted
2 cups pineapple chunks
1 cup green grapes
2 blue figs
BLEND.

– Enlighten Me Banana Date –

2 cups water
½ cup strawberries
1 peach, pitted
2 bananas (frozen or fresh)
1 pear
½ cup blueberries
6 large Medjool dates, pitted
BLEND.

– Enlighten Me Purple Rain –

1 cup frozen red dragon fruit, chunks (pitaya)
1 cup orange juice
1 cup pineapple chunks
2 cups green grapes
1 cup elderberry juice
1 cup blackberries
1 cup blueberries
BLEND.

– Enlighten Me Rockin' Reds –

2 cups red pomegranate juice
1 cup raspberries
1 orange, peeled
2 yellow kiwis, peeled
1 green pear, chunked
½ cup blackberries
BLEND.

– Enlighten Me Sweets –

3 cups coconut water
1 small red papaya, deseeded and peeled
1 large mango, peeled and pitted
3 baby bananas, peeled
¼ cup lime juice
2 figs
BLEND.

– Enlighten Me Orange –

6 blood oranges, juiced
2 oranges, peeled
2 yellow kiwis
1 pear
1 cup blackberries
BLEND.

– Enlighten Me Berries –

2 cups coconut water
2 cups strawberries
1½ cup raspberries
1 peach, deseeded
1 yellow kiwi, peeled
1 cup green grapes
2 cups blueberries
1½ cup blackberries
BLEND.

– Enlighten Me Melons –

1 quart watermelon pieces, deseeded
½ cantaloupe, peeled and deseeded
½ canary melon, peeled and deseeded
1 honeydew, peeled and deseeded
1 handful spearmint
BLEND.

– Enlighten Me Up –

2 cups water
1 quart strawberries
4 Valencia oranges, peeled
1 yellow kiwi, peeled
1 cup green grapes
1 cup blueberries
BLEND.

– Enlighten Me Baby –

2 cups coconut water
1 cup red grapes
1 cup papaya, deseeded and peeled
6 baby bananas, peeled
1 cup green grapes
2 cups purple figs
BLEND.

– Enlighten Me Coco Mint –

2 cups coconut water
½ red papaya, deseeded and peeled
1 ripe orange persimmon
1 pineapple, peeled, cored, and chunked
16 mint leaves
1 packet frozen dragon fruit (pitaya)
BLEND.

– Enlighten Me Slim –

2 cups coconut water
1 cup pomegranate seeds
1 cup cherries
1 orange, peeled
1 banana, peeled
1 cup spinach leaves
1 cup blueberries
BLEND.

– Enlighten Me Peachy –

2 cups blood-orange juice
1 banana
3 peaches
2 handfuls leafy greens (any kind)
2 purple plums, deseeded
BLEND.

– Enlighten Me Dragon –

2 cups red apple juice

1 orange, peeled

2 baby bananas, peeled

2 tablespoons Royal Spirulina powder

2 packets frozen dragon fruit

1 cup frozen wild blueberries

BLEND.

– Enlighten Me Green –

½ red onion

2 cups orange juice

1 lemon, juiced

2 green apples, cored

6 leaves romaine lettuce

3 celery sticks

1½ cups cilantro (pressed down)

1 cup blueberries

2 cloves garlic

BLEND.

– Enlighten Me Apple V-8 –

4 Fuji apples, cored
2 cups carrot juice
1 yellow heirloom tomato
2 handfuls baby spinach
2 kale leaves
½ cup blackberries
2 cloves garlic
½ jalapeño pepper
BLEND.

– Enlighten Me Sweet Sprouts –

2 red apples, cored
2 cups carrot juice
2 yellow kiwi
1 cucumber, peeled
1 handful broccoli sprouts
1 handful sunflower sprouts
BLEND.

– Enlighten Me Royal Spirulina –

2 cups water
1 cup strawberries
4 navel oranges
1 banana, peeled
1 tablespoon Royal Spirulina powder
1 packet frozen acai
BLEND.

– Enlighten Me Dandy –

2 cups water
1 red apple, cored
2 carrots, peeled
1 yellow apple, cored
1 cup dandelion greens, chopped
1 cup blueberries
2 Medjool dates, pitted
BLEND.

– Enlighten Me Eve –

1 red apple, cored
2 cups orange juice
1 yellow apple, cored
1 green apple, cored
1 packet frozen acai
BLEND.

Enlighten Me
7 Colors for 7 Days

Juice Fast

Freshly-prepared juices are advanced cleansers of the body. Not only are they one of the fastest ways to cleanse your body of unnatural substances, they are also the most effective way to alkalize your body and power up your immunity! In essence, what you're going to experience in the next seven days is an enzymatic, phytochemical-nutrient "blood transfusion!"

Choose a juicer: Preparing fresh organic juices requires a great juicer, one that gives you the highest nutrient yield. For this reason, Norman Walker created the Norwalk juicer, which grinds and presses the juice from plants. However, not only is the Norwalk juicer expensive, it is also very time consuming. So unless you travel to a great healing center where someone makes your juice for you, I suggest purchasing a "slow juicer."

These juicers actually make juice in record time—they are called *slow* only because of the slower, masticating movement of the inner workings. Slow juicers create less oxidation than a typical centrifugal juicer and produce a high nutrient yield. My favorite is the Hands-Free Slow Juicer AUTO10 made by Kuvings USA.

Choose your ingredients: Use high-quality, organic produce only. There's evidence to indicate that genetically engineered plant materials can actually cause cancer and other degenerative diseases. The genetic structure of these plants may have unintended mutations and cross-species corruption. Genetically modified plants also contain higher levels of crop pesticides, which are found both on the surface of the plant and internally. Fruits such as bananas, papayas, and some apples, are now genetically modified—unless you buy organic.

Choose your favorite juice recipes: Even though I am offering some of my favorite juice recipes, feel free to deviate from them and make up your own! You may want to purchase a book of juicing recipes like Norman Walker's classic *Fresh Vegetable and Fruit Juices.*

If you've never made juice before, don't be intimidated. It's simple:

> Step One: Wash and prepare ingredients.
> Step Two: Slowly add all ingredients to juicer.
> Step Three: Enjoy!

Keep in mind that organization is a huge factor in your success! Even though it's best to drink your juice immediately after juicing, it may be easier for you to juice twice a day, making a quart of juice to drink in the morning and then again in the afternoon. That means you'll be consuming two quarts of juice a day. If you feel you need more, simply juice more! I often suggest taking your body weight, dividing it by two, which gives you the perfect hydrating amount to drink each day.

Here are a few tips for juicing:
- Wash then cut your fruits and leafy greens the moment before you start making your juice. Fresh, raw fruits and leafy greens are alive and begin to oxidize the minute you cut them open. This means a loss of enzymes and nutrients if they sit around very long.

- If you're traveling or working outside your home, make your juices for the entire day first thing in the morning. Once made, pour each juice in a tightly sealed jar (I like mason jars). Keep the juices cool between periods of drinking to preserve nutrients. Then shake them up each time just before enjoying.

- Look ahead and keep the most often used fruits, greens, veggies, and herbs on hand, so you don't have to shop every day.

Juice fast recipes often include the following fruits:

Apples	Oranges	Pineapple
Lemon or Lime	Grapes	Grapefruit

Juice fast recipes often include the following vegetables:

Celery	Carrots	Kale
Cucumber	Spinach	Spinach

Juice fast recipes often include the following herbs and spices:

Ginger	Turmeric	Garlic
Mint	Jalapeño pepper	Broccoli Sprouts

Be sure to scrub, trim, destem, peel and slice all of your fruits and veggies as needed.

Enlighten Me Juice Recipes

– Enlighten Me Greens –

6 red chard leaves
2 yellow apples
6 celery stalks
2 large cucumbers
¼ cup parsley leaves
1-inch piece of ginger
JUICE.

– Enlighten Me Detox –

3 large beets
4 large carrots
2 yellow apples
1 lemon, whole
2-inch piece of ginger
2-inch jalapeño pepper
JUICE.

– Enlighten Me Eyes –

6 blood oranges

1 cup raspberries

4 carrots

1-inch piece of turmeric

½ lemon, whole

1 handful green leafy lettuce

JUICE.

– Enlighten Me Kidneys –

6 red apples

6 carrots

1-inch piece of turmeric

½ lemon, whole

1 handful parsley leaves

1 handful dandeliion leaves

JUICE.

– Enlighten Me Water –

½ gallon purified water

6 wedges pink grapefruit, peeled

1 small orange, peeled and sliced

½ lemon, whole and sliced

½ cucumber, sliced

4 peppermint leaves

Let sit for 2 hours.

– Enlighten Me Lymph –

6 red grapefruits, peeled
6 oranges, peeled
2 lemons, peeled
1 lime, peeled
1-inch piece of ginger
1-inch piece of turmeric
JUICE.

– Enlighten Me Fat Flush –

4 red grapefruits
4 navel oranges
1 lemon, whole
½ bunch celery
4 kale leaves
1-inch piece of ginger
JUICE.

– Enlighten Me Detoxifier –

6 large red apples
6 large beets
4 carrots
1 lemon, whole
½ jalapeño pepper
½ purple/black radish
JUICE.

– Enlighten Me Even More –

1 cayenne pepper
2 orange bell peppers
3 cups pineapple juice
1 lime, peeled
1-inch piece of ginger
JUICE.

– Enlighten Me Intestinal Flush –

6 red apples
6 carrots
2 lemons, peeled
1 handful spinach
1-inch piece of ginger
JUICE.

– Enlighten Me Clean –

6 large beets
4 large carrots
1 lemon, whole
½ bunch celery
½ or a whole jalapeño pepper
JUICE.

– Enlighten Me Please –

3 large lemons
8 large grapefruits
10 large oranges
JUICE.

– Enlighten Me Grapes –

1 quart red grapes
1-inch piece of turmeric
1 quart golden Muscat grapes
1 lemon, whole
1 quart green grapes
1 quart purple grapes
JUICE.

– Enlighten Me Antioxidants –

1 quart pomegranate seeds
2 ripe persimmons
4 yellow pears
1 handful spinach
1 cup blueberries
JUICE.

– Enlighten Me Granny –

6 red apples
4 carrots
6 yellow apples
4 Granny Smith apples
2 cups black cherries
JUICE.

– Enlighten Me Rainbow –

2 small beets
2 carrots
2 oranges
1 cup spinach
½ cup blueberries
1-inch piece of ginger
JUICE.

– Enlighten Me V-8 –

8 large beets
8 large carrots
2 large yellow heirloom tomatoes
½ bunch celery
1 handful spinach
1 handful parsley
¼ head purple cabbage
JUICE.

– Enlighten Me Heart –

1 quart red grapes
1 quart mango chunks
1 quart pineapple chunks
2 kiwis
1 quart green grapes
1 cup blueberries
JUICE.

– Enlighten Me More –

1 quart strawberries
3 large navel oranges
1 quart pineapple chunks
½ bunch celery
1 cup blackberries
JUICE.

– Enlighten Me Fire Flush –

6 granny smith apples
1 lemon, whole
1 large cucumber
½ bunch celery
1 handful parsley
1 handful cilantro
1 jalapeño pepper
1-inch turmeric
1-inch piece of ginger
JUICE.

– Enlighten Me Liver –

6 large beets
2 large carrots
4 yellow apples
1 lemon, whole
1 handful dandelion greens
1-inch piece of ginger
1 jalapeño pepper
JUICE.

– Enlighten Me Blood –

2 cups red radishes
½ cayenne pepper
6 navel oranges
6 large carrots
2 yellow pears
½ bunch celery
1 handful sunflower sprouts
1 handful parsley
JUICE.

CLEANSE AND REGENERATIVE BOOSTERS

Power up your *New Earth Fast* with four power boosters that will amp up the effectiveness of your fast, whether eating fruit or drinking smoothies or juices. So if you're ready to "cleanse out the old" so you can "shift into the new," let's get started.

There are four power boosters to include with your fast: (1) lobelia tincture, (2) cayenne tincture, and (3) your favorite gut flush formula,

To begin, the great herbalist Dr. John Christopher (1909–1983) believed that lobelia and cayenne tinctures should be in everyone's medicine cabinet because, together, they hold the power to "cure" almost anything!

Lobelia is a *water herb* and cayenne is a *fire herb*.

Lobelia is a relaxant and relaxes the membrane of cells so toxic wastes are more easily released; cayenne is a stimulant and increases circulation in order to move toxic wastes out of the blood and lymph. After understanding both of their dynamic properties, I now view them as the *baptism of water and fire!*

CLEANSE OUT THE OLD with Lobelia

Lobelia inflata is an annual or biennial plant considered to be one of the most valuable herbal remedies ever discovered. It has been historically used and appreciated for a number of functions, including the removal of toxins, craving control, and perhaps most notably, its ability to relieve problematic respiratory symptoms.

In the 1800s, both Native Americans and medical doctors also used lobelia to induce vomiting in cases of food poisoning. For this reason, lobelia was sometimes called "puke weed." But not only are its purging effects physical; it also helps you to "cleanse out the old" limiting beliefs and false perceptions that come forth out of the Ego-Mind!

Needless to say, there are some precautions to be taken with lobelia. Dosages are tricky for two reasons: (1) the potency of preparations varies and, (2) the response can vary widely between individuals. While lobelia has fabulous healing properties, more is not better. Everyone is different, so it's up to you to monitor and regulate your own dose. The *more* toxic you are, the *less* lobelia you will be able to tolerate.

When using lobelia extract, start with ½ dropperful in a ½ cup of water, 3 times a day, and eventually work up to a dropperful 4 times a day. Just be mindful and work with lobelia's deep cleansing abilities, as well as listening to the voice of your body. I promise that it will let you know when enough is enough! After all, lobelia didn't get the nickname "puke weed" for nothing!

Incorporating the ho'oponopono forgiveness process every time you take a dose of lobelia is life changing. Remember, the ho'oponopono forgiveness process means *to make right*. It also means *to be released from; to let go of; or to clean your consciousness of limiting beliefs and false perceptions*.

SHIFT INTO THE NEW with Cayenne

While cayenne has been used for thousands of years as a culinary herb to spice up our food, the master herbalist Dr. Christopher considered cayenne to be the greatest herbal medicine in the world.

Cayenne is best known as the circulatory herb, because it increases blood flow to every "nook and cranny," thus helping to move wastes out of circulation. Not only does it adjust blood pressure toward normalcy by dissolving accumulations of sticky mucus that obstructs blood flow; it also helps to repair the elasticity of arteries and veins.

Cayenne has even been accredited with stopping heart attacks when symptoms first present themselves. It also works in the digestive system, rebuilding tissue in the stomach and intestinal lining, producing natural warmth, and stimulating the peristaltic action of the intestines for improved assimilation and elimination.

If you notice a burning or belly-cramping sensation when taking therapeutic doses of cayenne, you may want to invite the "fiery burn" (baptism of fire) to do its transformational work. Thank it as it burns away the thick, layered veils of mucus that have hindered you from creating the desires of your heart.

When using cayenne extract, add ½ dropperful of cayenne extract to a cup of warm water. Warm water allows for deeper penetration, thus deeper cleansing. Drink this mixture 3 to 4 times a day. Again, adjust the dosage according to how deeply your body is ready to clean out the old so it can shift into the new. You may want to go slowly at first, then after a few days, accelerate the process with more cayenne and go for it!

Incorporating the I AM prayer every time you take a dose of cayenne will change the course of your life forever. Remember, the I AM prayer means *to affirm; to proclaim; to demand, to shift into the new;* and ultimately *to create* a new world within and around you!

MOVE IT OUT with your favorite Gut Flush

The need to "flush our gut" is greater today than ever before. That's because most people are taking in more toxic chemicals than ever before through polluted air, water and food. Researchers now know that our gut houses approximately 70 percent of the body's immune cells. In essence, our gut functions as our immune system's "control tower" while simultaneously serving as a digestive, nutrient uptake organ.

In addition to various types of immune cells, the gut also contains approximately 500 types of gut bacteria, averaging about 100 trillion organisms in total. This is called the *microbiome*. Our gut microbiome may weigh as much as five pounds. These microorganisms help to digest our food, regulate our immune system, protect us against disease-causing pathogens, and produce vitamins, including B12, thiamine, riboflavin, and vitamin K.

Think of the gut as your body's "exodus point." If toxic substances and undigested food particles are allowed to accumulate, your gut is subject to becoming a breeding ground for the creation of x-y-z disease. In fact, most holistic-health experts believe that a clogged gut is the root cause of almost every disease known.

Remember, you don't "catch" diseases, you create them! Thus, the maxim... "death begins in the colon."

Note: If you're juicing, I highly recommend using the saltwater intestinal flush to cleanse your intestinal tract, mostly because of a lack of fiber.

Saltwater Gut Flush

In ancient Hawaiian purification practices, saltwater was used for its medicinal properties to cleanse the body by flushing out toxins, waste material, and parasites from the colon. Today, the Celtic Sea Salt® company has manufactured a pure seawater salt called Makai Pure®

This salt is as close as you can get to the original salt used in the Hawaiian purification ceremonies. Harvested in Hawaii, this seawater salt is sourced from deep ocean currents with higher salinity. It is then placed in a controlled greenhouse environment to dry, resulting in a beautiful, pure sea salt packed with top-tier minerals and flavor.

How to Make Your Makai Saltwater Flush:

- The Recipe: Dissolve two teaspoons of Makai Celtic Sea Salt® in one quart of warm water.
- Drink Immediate: Drink the warm mixture as quickly as possible on an empty stomach.
- Wait 30 minutes after drinking before consuming anything else.
- Potential Effects: The saltwater solution acts as a mild laxative, encouraging bowel movements.
- Be Prepared: Stay near a restroom, as the mixture may produce a laxative effect.

Note: Before attempting a saltwater flush, especially if you have underlying health conditions or are pregnant or breastfeeding, consult with a healthcare professional.

SHIFT with Alkalize Yourself

Our body's ability to buffer acids is critical to our very survival. Let me explain how this works. Our body has a buffering system that acts much like a sponge. If the sponge's ability to absorb acids reaches its maximum capacity, the pH of our body's fluids may drop rapidly to more dangerous levels of acidity. If this happens, our buffering system is forced to call upon our body's *alkaline reserves*.

Alkaline reserves refer to a storehouse of organic electrolyte-minerals in organs, glands, and bones that, when needed, supports the buffering system. The most important of these organic electrolyte-minerals are sodium, potassium, calcium, and magnesium. The primary and most important of these four is organic sodium.

Organic sodium is not the same as inorganic sodium, such as the sodium chloride found in most processed table salts. The term organic, in this case, refers to sodium that comes from plant foods.

Organic sodium is the primary electrolyte in our extracellular fluid—the blood and lymph that surrounds and feeds our cells. Potassium is the primary electrolyte in our intracellular fluid—the fluid inside our cells. The balance between these two fluids—extracellular and intracellular—is the key to a dynamic pH equilibrium. Together, they create a "cellular pump" that carries nutrients into our cells and wastes out.

While the balance between these two fluids is subtle and complex, it is the answer to maintaining our body's nature alkaline design. If our "inner seas" become deficient in organic sodium, our body's innate intelligence will draw upon alkaline reserves out of various systems to make sure the proper balance is maintained. This is similar to drawing money out of your bank without making any deposits!

To make sure your "inner seas" have adequate amounts of organic sodium, I have created an organic plant-based product high in organic sodium called *Alkalize Yourself!* If this product isn't available yet, look for the following dehydrated organic powders that are the highest in organic sodium that you can take: Celery powder, beet powder, spirulina powder, and goji powder. These organic powders are concentrated to make sure that you are, or become, the *alkaline you* that you were designed to be!

Royal Spirulina

Spirulina is a type of blue-green algae that grows in both freshwater and saltwater environments. Often referred to as a superfood, it is packed with essential nutrients. As a supplement, spirulina has been shown to offer a variety of potential health benefits, including improved gut health, enhanced immune function, blood sugar balance, pH regulation, and a reduction in inflammation. The spirulina I recommend is called Royal Spirulina.

Why "Royal" Spirulina?

> (1) Superior Cultivation Process: It's grown in patented bioreactors, ensuring a controlled, contaminant-free environment, unlike open-pond spirulina, which is exposed to pollution and inconsistent conditions.

> (2) Unique Washing Method: Royal Spirulina uses a patented washing process that preserves the cell wall, maintaining maximum nutrient bioavailability, especially phycocyanin, the powerful blue antioxidant.

> (3) Freeze-Dried, Not Spray-Dried: Many spirulina products

are spray-dried using high heat, which destroys nutrients. Royal Spirulina is freeze-dried, preserving its full nutritional profile and enzymatic activity.

(3) Higher Phycocyanin Content: Phycocyanin is the key antioxidant responsible for spirulina's health benefits. Thanks to its specialized processing, Royal Spirulina contains exceptionally high levels compared to standard spirulina.

(4) Purity & Transparency: Unlike low-quality spirulina, especially from China, which may contain heavy metals, contaminants, and fillers, Royal Spirulina is clean, pure, and tested to ensure premium quality.

By combining cutting-edge technology, purity, and a commitment to superior nutrition, Royal Spirulina is in a league of its own.

The New Earth Fasting Lifestyle

While fasting, forgiveness and prayer are the most important things you can do during the 7-day new moon phase, there are a few lifestyle habits that can assist the effectiveness of your fast. These habits can be highly beneficial even beyond your monthly fasting period.

Scrub it out!

The skin is our body's largest and most complex organ. Some call it the body's third kidney because of its role in eliminating wastes from the body. *Exfoliation* is the removal of dead skin cells from the surface of the skin. There are two ways to exfoliate your skin: dry skin brushing and salt scrubs.

Dry skin brushing is the practice of using a dry skin brush to brush the surface of your skin. Before stepping in the shower or bath, brush for about 3 to 5 minutes to scrub away dead skin. This practice was popularized by author, teacher, and healer Dr. Paavo Airola of Finland. Dr. Airola believed dry-skin brushing to be an essential part of any cleansing and regenerative program. The sheer mechanical action of dry-skin brushing unclogs our pores, which allows toxins to exit through the skin more freely. It also helps detoxify us by increasing effective blood circulation and stimulating better lymph flow.

Salt scrubs are another great way to exfoliate your skin. Salt has cleansing qualities, so it's helpful for maintaining pathogen-free skin. As with dry skin brushing, the abrasive friction between the salt and the surface of the skin helps to remove dead skin cells, unclog the pores, which invigorates the circulation of blood and allows toxins to exit.

Bathe it out!
After you've scrubbed your skin, there's nothing more relaxing and detoxifying than a nice, hot bath with Celtic bath salts. Because of its high mineral content, a Celtic Sea Salt® bath helps to stimulate blood flow while drawing out acids and toxins. The bathing method is simple…

- Make sure you won't be disturbed for at least an hour. It's time to relax! Light a few candles and play your favorite relaxing music.
- Fill your bath with warm to hot water. The heat level is up to you. However, the hotter, the better!
- Add 2 to 3 hefty handfuls of Celtic bath salts. Do not use regular table salt because beneficial minerals have been removed through refinement.

- Feel free to add a few drops of pure essential oils for aromatherapy purposes. Lavender is a great choice, as it will also help you to destress.
- For an even deeper detox, try adding a cup of apple cider vinegar and ¼ cup powdered ginger to your bath.
- Soak for 20 to 30 minutes. You can use this time to cleanse out any accumulated toxic wastes and limiting beliefs so you can shift into the new you!
- For the best results, air dry when you get out of the bath. You may use a towel for your hair and put a robe on, but do not towel dry. If possible, don't even shower for the next 24 hours.

Sweat it out!

Sweat it out with the ultimate infrared sauna experience called Sauna Space. With Sauna Space, you'll have the best of both worlds. First it includes full spectrum infrared light along with warm, soothing incandescent light bulbs that helps promote cellular repair and overall wellness. Together, these innovative technologies in this unique infrared sauna works synergistically to provide a transformative wellness experience to help you clear your mind, heal your body, and energize your spirit. This technology is also designed with EMF shielding that protects you so you can relax and rejuvenate with peace of mind.

While you're sweating it out, be sure to keep yourself hydrated with lots of water. But not just any water...

Hydrate it out!

Water, in its natural state, is transformative. Natural water is alive, clean and structured the way nature intended, thus having the ability to hydrate you. Unnatural water is dead, polluted, unstructured and ineffective in its ability to hydrate you.

Water that flows in springs is considered "structured" as it has the ability to flow through its natural spiraling springs. Water that flows unnaturally through pipes and out of our tap or shower is considered "unstructured," mostly because it no longer has a natural spiraling flow. Tap water is also contaminated with toxic chemicals such as mercury, lead, fluoride, chlorine, pharmaceuticals, herbicides, pesticides, and volatile organic compounds (VOCs). Therefore, finding the right way to purify and restructure the water we drink and bathe in is of utmost importance.

While there are various ways to treat drinking water, such as reverse osmosis, distillers, and filters, each ranging in cost and quality, these water technologies focus on purification only. They do not address the primary reason for drinking water—the ability to hydrate you!

Studies have shown that being just 2 percent dehydrated leads to measurable cognitive loss, and being 10 percent dehydrated can lead to chronic illness.

Lawrence E. Armstrong, an international expert on hydration, says,

> *"Our thirst sensation doesn't really appear until we are 1 or 2 percent dehydrated. By then dehydration is already setting in and starting to impact how our mind and body perform."*

Have you ever consumed a lot of water yet still felt thirsty? This is because at the cellular level, the water you're drinking is not being absorbed. We are told that we need to drink 8 glasses of water a day. But what if the *amount* of water isn't the *real* issue?

Most of us are familiar with the three phases of water—liquid, solid (ice), and gas (steam). But the discovery of structured water introduced a fourth phase; the phase in which water is more organized and able to generate electricity at the molecular level, which allows for faster, deeper absorption. In order to cleanse deeply, we have to have watery fluids that move and absorb deeply.

Anthropologist Gina Bria, Founder of the Hydration Foundation and coauthor of *Quench*, discovered that people living in indigenous deserts were better hydrated than the average American, simply because they were eating liquid-containing raw plants. Plants are 99 percent structured water!

She says…

> *"A diet high in fresh fruits and veggies, leafy greens and herbs is a powerful source of better hydration than water alone."*

According to the Hydration Foundation, 99 percent of the molecules that make up the human body are water! New research is showing us how the health of our cells is directly tied to the structure of the water inside. The goal, then, should be to give your body water that is clean, hydrating and life-promoting.

Consider the Lourdes springs in France. Lourdes is home to one of the most famous healing shrines in the world. Many of the 4 to 6 million visitors a year go there to drink and bathe in the water in hopes of seeking a cure. Scientists have studied this spring water since the late 1800s, hoping to unlock its mysteries and documenting the water's miraculous results.

A company called *Spring Aqua* has developed their version of Lourdes's water through mimicking the rock layers, geology, and other properties outlined in scientific studies. As a result, they have created a complete water-hydration technology they call *Ecosystem in a Box*. This is the water I drink and recommend. You can find this amazing water machine on my website: tonitoney.com

Bounce it out!
The idea of bouncing on a rebounder for better health has been around for a long time, but it gained popularity in the 1980s when NASA studied its benefits while trying to find an effective way to help astronauts recover bone and muscle mass after being in space. Astronauts can lose as much as 15 percent of their bone and muscle mass from only 14 days in zero gravity, so NASA needed a way to help reverse this damage.

Rebounding was the answer. They discovered that rebounding uses the forces of acceleration and deceleration, which provide benefits on a cellular level at a greater rate than other forms of exercise. In essence, the up-and-down action of rebounding makes use of the earth's gravitational force in rebuilding bone and muscle more quickly than anything else.

But rebounding is not just about building bone and muscle mass. Gently bouncing on a rebounder (mini-trampoline) is a great way to move your lymph. Bouncing creates an intermittent gravitational pull on the waters of your body (much like moon cycles), which opens and closes the valves in the lymph ducts, thereby increasing circulation, lymphatic drainage, immune function, emotional health, and much more.

To further activate the flow of lymph while bouncing, incorporate the power of your breath through short, accelerated, deep breathing. While gently bouncing with toes remaining on the rebounder, take three quick breaths in, hold for 3 to 6 seconds, then three quick breaths out, hold for another 3 to 6 seconds.

There are several different models of rebounders on the market to choose from. My favorite is made by Leaps and Rebounds. Their bungee suspension system maximizes the bounce, which gives us the best lymphatic-pumping workout in the world. And the great news is… it's very affordable!

Rebounding is also lots of fun! Simply put on your favorite music and start bouncing! What's more awesome than that? You can find this amazing rebounder on my website: tonitoney.com

Breathe it out!
When I finally grasped the notion that it's *truly* the great I AM <u>THAT</u> I AM who is breathing us, my life changed forever. My temple worship was taking place within me instead of within a place of brick and mortar. As I worshipped and loved the Creator of my life with all of my mind, heart and soul, the shift of the ages began to anchor itself as a visceral reality. I began living in an endless sea of change… that of "letting go of the old" and "taking hold of the new." It was truly a metamorphosis "born again" experience.

Like the caterpillar who crawls upon the earth, then stops eating, hangs upside down from a twig or leaf, and eventually morphs into a butterfly who is free to fly above the earth, we, too, have the ability within us to go through a similar process during the 7-day new moon phase.

As I breathe in, I give thanks to Spirit, who is my Creator, my life force, director and intelligence of my body, for being my all, my everything, my life. As I breathe out, I let go of (forgive) any part of my mind that once believed that I was separate from the great I AM <u>THAT</u> I AM.

With this new way of breathing, I could feel my body becoming less and less dense, as though it were dissolving itself into Spirit, which is why I now call this focused, transformational breathing *the breath of translation;* a way to breathe ourselves out of the old and into the new; a way to shift from physical consciousness into spiritual consciousness!

I began to take notice of the quality of air I was breathing, wanting it to be as pure as possible. Unfortunately, the air in most of our homes is filled with toxic substances—formaldehyde, asbestos, nitrogen dioxide, carbon monoxide, pesticides, mold, volatile organic compounds (VOC's), etc. I searched for the best indoor air purifier. The one I have in my home and recommend is the Aerus Air Purification Systems.

The technology used in this compact unit is called ActivePure, developed by NASA scientists to eliminate ethylene gas onboard the International Space Station. This powerful nature-based technology has been scientifically proven to destroy airborne and surface viruses, black mold, fungus, volatile organic compounds, and bacteria such as MRSA, E-coli, and Staph. Recent testing conducted by an independent FDA-compliant laboratory, MRI Global, established a 99.98 percent surface kill rate of live SARS-CoV-2 (COVID)!

Sunbathe it out!

Sunbathing is one of the most important things you can do for your health, especially while fasting. Unfortunately, most of us have lost our personal relationship with the sun. We've gone from worshipping it to rejecting its gifts, both in the religious sense as well as in the bronzed sense. While every living thing on our planet is dependent upon the light of the sun, we've been made to believe that it is our enemy, that sunbathing is dangerous. It has become something to be blocked out or even avoided.

It is my belief that when the "inner seas" of our body (blood and lymph) are like a *pure stream,* bathing in the light of the sun is one of the most powerful things we can do. If, on the other hand, our waters are toxic, acidic and low in oxygen, sunlight can indeed trigger negative immune responses.

So, if your saliva pH is acidic, I would recommend sunbathing around 9 AM for only 20 minutes at a time until your "inner seas" are less toxic.

In general, you can make sunbathing safer by consuming an array of colorful, phytochemical-nutrient-rich fruits and veggies, which are *high* in antioxidants, and avoiding foods that are *low* in antioxidants, such as meat, dairy, and processed foods. Antioxidants increase your skin's ability to absorb sunlight and defend against the breakdown of skin cells exposed to the sun. Fasting on an array of colorful, freshly-prepared, phytochemical-nutrient-rich organic smoothies or juices, or simply eating fruit during the 7-day new moon phase will provide your body with the protection it needs against harmful rays.

When your skin is exposed to sunlight (without the use of sunblock), it makes vitamin D from cholesterol, which is why Vitamin D has long been deemed the "sunshine vitamin." When the sun's ultraviolet B (UVB) rays triggers the cholesterol in the skin cells, they provide the energy for vitamin D synthesis to occur. A new research study at the University of Chicago is now showing that high vitamin D levels may be your greatest protection against most every virus or pathogenic germ. Sadly, it's estimated that more than 40 percent of American adults have a vitamin D deficiency.

According to Zane Kime, M.D., in his book *Sunlight Could Save Your Life*, sunlight has the power to strengthen the body's resistance to infectious diseases, increase the oxygen capacity of blood, improve stress tolerance, lower blood sugar, and offer a host of further health benefits.

Gina Bria, of the Hydration Foundation, tells us that...

> *"Sunlight exposure is one of the key ways to structure water inside of you."*

The best time to sunbathe is before 10 AM or after 3 PM—times when the ultraviolet (UV) rays are less intense. Start with 10 minutes either in the early morning (9 AM) or late afternoon (4 PM). Add a few more minutes each day until you have a healthy, bronze tan. The less covering you have on, without the use of sunblock, the better.

The Schedule

During your 7-day *New Earth Fast*, it is not necessary to take your usual supplements, so feel free to set them aside for now. If you're taking medications, be sure to consult with your trusted holistic physician or health-care provider before starting the fast. Three nights before the new moon, take your chosen herbal *gut flush* product to begin the elimination process.

On this program, we'll also be incorporating the principles of intermittent or circadian rhythm fasting, which means no calories during a 4 to 8 hour window, not even from fruit.

6:00 AM
According to Traditional Chinese Medicine, the highest energy flow for the large intestine meridian occurs between the hours of 5 AM and 7 AM, which makes 6 AM the perfect time to rise and shine!

Before you drink water or brush your teeth, check your saliva pH and write it down. This will give you your pH baseline. You will *not* need to check it again during the fast. After you've checked your saliva pH, enjoy 2 cups of warm, structured water with a squeeze of lemon to help move your bowels.

7:00 AM
Take your first dose of lobelia and cayenne. Squeeze 11 drops of lobelia extract into a half cup of warm water and drink it up. Remember, lobelia is the "letting go of" herb, so this is a great time to use the ho'oponopono forgiveness process to cleanse your consciousness of any limiting beliefs and false perceptions you may have.

Wait a few minutes, then add 7 drops of cayenne extract to a half cup of warm water and drink it up. Yes, it's going to be hot, stimulating and cleansing! While you're on fire is a great time to affirm and "take hold of" the desires of your heart by using the I AM prayer.

Affirm: "I AM <u>THAT</u> I AM." You fill in <u>THAT</u> which you desire.

Choose only one ho'oponopono forgiveness request
and one I AM affirmative prayer a day.

Sit quietly, or lie back down in bed, with eyes closed, for the next 30 minutes (make the time!), consciously connecting to the great I AM <u>THAT</u> I AM through the power of your breath. Slowly breath in your affirmative prayer of the day, then slowly breath out your ho'oponopono forgiveness request of the day. When you begin each day this way, magic happens!

8:00 AM
Exercise! Move your lymph! Do some rebounding.

8:30 AM
Brush your skin and enjoy a detox bath or far-infrared sauna. Repeat your ho'oponopono forgiveness request and affirmative prayer during this time.

9:30 AM
Sunbathe for 15 to 20 minutes without sunscreen. Continue to repeat your ho'oponopono forgiveness request and affirmative prayer during this time.

10:00 AM
Take your second dose of lobelia and cayenne extract while repeating your ho'oponopono forgiveness request and your affirmative prayer.

11:00 AM

Prepare your smoothie, juice or fruit of the day, depending on the level of cleansing you're working with. If you have a busy schedule, feel free to prepare your drink of choice for the entire day, enjoying it as you have time and desire to do so.

12:00 PM

Drink your smoothie, juice or simply eat lots of fruit.

2:00 PM

Take your third dose of lobelia and cayenne extract while repeating your ho'oponopono forgiveness request and affirmative prayer.

3:30 PM

Drink another smoothie or juice or simply eat some fruit.

4:30 PM

Take your fourth dose of lobelia and cayenne extract while repeating your ho'oponopono forgiveness request and your affirmative prayer.

6:00 PM

Drink another smoothie or juice or simply eat some fruit.

7:00 PM

Time for a short, inner-reflective walk.

9:00 PM

Take the recommended amount of your favorite "gut flush" as written on the bottle just before bedtime. Sometimes I take a little more to really get my morning bowels moving! Then repeat your daily ho'oponopono forgiveness request and affirmative prayer as you drift off into the world you have always dreamt of.

So, if you're ready to shift from physical consciousness to spiritual consciousness so your soul can once again be free to be everything it was created to be, a 7-day new moon fast every month is for you!

The time has come.
The time to become SPIRIT-FILLED is now.
The New Earth Fast is how!

NEW EARTH FAST

– 6 –
WHAT TO EAT AFTER THE FAST
Eat to Enlighten Yourself

Now that you've completed the *New Earth Fast,* how you break your fast is extremely important. To start eating a diet high in acid-forming foods such as meat, dairy, bread, or processed foods after your fast would be disastrous to your newly cleansed, alkalized "inner seas" and digestive system. These foods are what I call "slow exit foods," simply because they are slow to digest, assimilate, and eliminate. They are also void of phytochemical light energy. On the other hand, raw fruits and vegetables are what I call "fast exit foods" simply because they are easy to digest, assimilate, and eliminate. They are also replete with phytochemical light energy.

Much like a caterpillar that has the ability to shed its skin during the transformational shift into a beautiful butterfly, we also have the ability to shed our mortal skin during the transformational shift in a beautiful, spiritualized body. Such a transformational shift, for both, can only take place when our bodies are ready! For us, fasting on an array of colorful, photochemical-nutrient-rich plant foods every month during the 7-day new moon phase, will make a huge difference in our ability to make the shift with ease and grace.

EAT RIGHT FOR YOUR ANATOMICAL TYPE

Carolus Linnaeus (1707-1778), the great taxonomist who established scientific methods for classifying plants and animals, recognized that humans are mostly fruit eaters by design. Linnaeus is believed to have said...

> *"Man's structure, internal and external, compared with that of the other animals, shows that fruit and succulent vegetables are his natural food."*

Let's take a closer look at a simple dental visual that sums up why Linnaeus believed this:

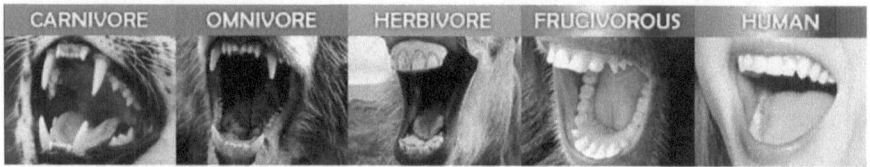

In terms of anatomy, it is very clear where humans fit in. In essence, a cow wasn't designed to eat a fish or a chicken; it was designed to eat grass. Likewise, a human wasn't designed to eat a cow, chicken or grass; we were designed to eat plant-based foods, especially fruit. In essence, we were never designed to eat the meat of an animal or any kind of animal-based foods.

The China Study (2005) documents the results of a 20-year research project directed by medical researchers T. Colin Campbell and Thomas M. Campbell II, in a partnership between Cornell University, Oxford University, and the Chinese Academy of Preventive Medicine. The research project revealed that people who primarily ate animal-based foods developed more chronic diseases than people who primarily ate plant-based foods. In fact, their research revealed a significant amount of evidence that links a diet high in protein, particularly animal protein, to chronic degenerative diseases.

They went so far as to say...

> *"Even relatively small intakes of animal-based foods were associated with adverse effects."*

To test his theory about animal-based foods, such as dairy products, Dr. Campbell fed two groups of rats a diet with different amounts of casein, the main protein in dairy products. After twelve weeks, all of the rats eating a diet of 20 percent casein had a greatly increased level of early cancer tumor growth while rats eating a 5 percent casein diet showed no evidence of cancer yet. He discovered that cancer growth could be turned on and off just by adjusting the level of casein intake.

Still, you may be asking yourself, so where do I get my protein?

My answer to that question is...

> Where does a carnivorous lion get theirs? ANIMALS!
> Where does an herbivorous cow get theirs? GRASS!
> Where does a frugivorous chimpanzee get theirs? FRUIT!

One of the most common myths about a plant-based diet is that you will not get enough protein. The outdated myth that we have to consume an animal for our daily protein requirements has been completely debunked. Although protein is certainly an essential nutrient that plays many key roles in the way our bodies function, we do not need huge quantities of it. In fact, fruits and vegetables contain the perfect amounts of protein, which can be compared to the amounts of protein in mother's milk, which is approximately 2.5 grams.

For your plant-based diet protein concerns, please consider the following:

AMOUNT OF PROTEIN IN FRUIT

Avocado	One medium-size contains 4.02 grams of protein.
Banana	One medium-size contains 1.29 grams of protein.
Blackberries	One cup contains 2 grams of protein.
Dates	One cup contains 3.6 grams of protein.
Grapefruit	One cup contains 1.45 grams of protein.
Grapes	One cup contains 1.09 grams of protein.
Mango	One without peel contains 1.06 grams of protein.
Mulberries	One cup contains 2.02 grams of protein.
Orange	One medium-size contains 1.23 grams of protein.
Passion fruit	One cup contains 5.19 grams of protein.
Peach	One medium-size (with skin) contains 1.36 grams of protein.
Plum	One cup contains 1.15 grams of protein.
Pomegranate	One contains 4.71 grams of protein.
Raspberries	One cup contains 1.48 grams of protein.
Tomato	One medium-size contains 1.08 grams of protein.
Watermelon	One medium wedge contains 1.74 grams of protein.

AMOUNT OF PROTEIN IN VEGETABLES

Alfalfa-sprouted	One cup contains 1.32 grams of protein.
Artichoke	One cooked without salt contains 3.47 grams of protein.
Asparagus	One-half cup cooked contains 2.16 grams of protein.
Bok Choy	One cup cooked without salt contains 2.65 grams of protein.
Broccoli	One cup cooked without salt contains 3.71 grams of protein.
Brussels Sprouts	One cup cooked without salt contains 3.98 grams of protein.
Butternut squash	One cup cooked without salt contains 1.84 grams of protein.
Cauliflower	One cup cooked without salt contains 2.28 grams of protein.
Celery	One cup cooked without salt contains 1.25 grams of protein.
French beans	One cup cooked without salt contains 12.48 grams of protein.
Kale	One cup cooked without salt contains 2.47 grams of protein.
Okra	One cup cooked without salt contains 3 grams of protein.
Parsnip	One cup cooked without salt contains 2.06 grams of protein.
Potatoes	One medium-size without salt contains 4.33 grams of protein.
Sweet potatoes	One medium baked contains 2.29 grams of protein.
Swiss chard	One cup cooked without salt contains 3.29 grams of protein.

When considering the whole dietary "eat this, no eat that" mayhem, the primary thought to consider is that our anatomical design is mostly that of a frugivorous chimpanzee. We are not carnivores by natural design; therefore, we do not have to eat the flesh of an animal to get our protein needs met!

Consider the chimpanzee's natural diet:

> Fruit (68 percent), leaves (11 percent), seeds (7 percent), insects (6 percent), flowers, pith and mammals (2 percent each), and bark (1 percent). Living in nature, their diet is uncooked and unprocessed. Rarely do you ever see chimpanzees, bonobos (pygmy chimpanzees), and orangutans eating animals.

While we are obviously not completely identical to chimpanzees and other apes, we are close enough to consider our physiological similarities, and how we should relate to our food choices. If we would observe chimpanzees in their natural habitat, we would be able to learn a great deal by simply watching them make their food choices.

Anthropologist Dr. Katharine Milton, professor at the University of California, Berkeley, asserts that many characteristics of modern primates, including humans, derive from our early ancestors' practice of taking most of its food from a tropical canopy. Food eaten by humans today, especially those consumed in industrially advanced nations, bears little resemblance to the plant-based diets anthropoids (monkeys, apes, and humans) have favored since their emergence. The widespread prevalence of diet-related health problems, particularly in highly industrialized nations, suggests that many humans are not eating in a manner compatible with their biology.

Dr. Milton concludes...

> *"Such findings lend support to the suspicion that many health problems common in technologically advanced nations may result, at least in part, from a mismatch between the diets we now eat and*

those to which our bodies became adapted over millions of years."

Therefore, I am advocating a diet much like that of our closest relatives, the chimpanzee and orangutan; however, with the following caveats:

- On occasion a chimpanzee might eat a few insects or a very small animal; however, this is not the norm, and definitely should not be ours.
- Humans are tropical beings by design. We were never meant to live where a variety of fruit trees don't blossom and produce fruit year-round. However, if you live in a place where fruit trees don't produce fruit year-round, a modified plant-based diet may be necessary, even if not ideal.
- Shifting back to our original, natural way of eating needs to be a slow and steady process.

The primary reason I suggest a slow, steady transition is to allow our bodies and minds time to adjust to a new way of eating. After all, we're not just cleaning toxic wastes out of our bodies from years of eating unnatural foods, but we are also cleaning limiting beliefs out of our minds from years of thinking unnatural thoughts. For these reasons, I have created *Seven New Earth Food Principles* that will support your body and mind for the shift of the ages!

Seven New Earth Food Principles

1. Consume whole, organic plant foods
2. Eat the right types of salt, oil and sugar
3. Eat locally grown, seasonal foods
4. Combine your foods properly
5. Follow the circadian rhythm

6. Feast while you fast
7. Eat your chosen *fuel food* plan

New Earth Food Principle #1
Consume Whole, Organic Plant Foods

The first New Earth Food Principle is to consume lots of whole, organic plant foods. Organic plant foods alkalize and oxygenize the "inner seas" of our bodies like nothing else. Just as plants saturate our planet's atmosphere with lots of oxygen, when we eat lots of organic plant foods, they also saturate our body's atmosphere with lots of oxygen. By consuming the foods you were originally designed to eat, foods that support your natural alkaline design, you'll be shifting from the "old you" into the "new you."

That means, you'll be consuming all of the organic fruits and vegetables you can eat, along with small amounts of nuts and seeds. These are the foods that come from seed-bearing plants, as proposed in the book of Genesis, as the perfect food for humans. Thus, no more frozen dinners in a package or fast-food meals in a box. Instead, you'll have fun in the kitchen creating new menu ideas for your new life. Or, you can simply follow my easy-to-make *fuel food* whole-food plant ideas as presented in New Earth Food Principle #7 towards the end of this chapter.

Always Choose Organic
When purchasing produce, always choose organic! Organically-grown fruits and vegetables are mostly void of toxic pollutants, such

as pesticides and herbicides, versus conventionally-grown toxic produce. Conventional farming refers to a more profit point of view, having very little concern for the health of the earth's ecology or the ecology of the human body. Conventional farmers use synthetic, toxic chemicals to fertilize soil and control weeds and insects, and more often than not, they also use toxic genetically engineered seeds. Whereas organic farmers opt for less harmful growing methods, such as manure or compost fertilizers and conscious crop rotation. The great news is that they never use genetically engineered seeds. In addition, organic produce has also been found to be substantially higher in nutrients than conventionally grown produce.

Few of us stop to think about the amount of chemical residue that is taken up by the plant foods we eat, let alone calculate the accumulated build-up of years of exposure to our bodies. While some believe that the benefits of pesticides outweigh any potential health risks, research suggests otherwise. To the sensitive, even the slightest amount of pesticide exposure can manifest as respiratory symptoms, gastrointestinal disease, headache, dizziness, confusion, skin problems, eye problems, and many other non-specific conditions.

For a more visual representation of the difference between organically-grown and commercially-grown crops, check out Walter Danzer's book, *The Invisible Power Within Foods*. Magnifications of the tissues of organically grown fruits and vegetables show clear structural organization. The tissues of nonorganic foods shows incoherence and a lack of structural integrity—the beginnings of ecological breakdown for the plants as well as for those who eat them.

Consume Lots of Raw, Living Plant Foods

Eating a diet high in raw, living foods is definitely the highest and best way to prepare your physical body for the shift of the ages. If 75 to 100 percent of your total food consumption consists of raw, living foods, you are considered what some call a "raw foodist." This simply means that the majority of the foods you're eating are in their natural, raw, whole-food, organic state—foods that are unprocessed and mostly uncooked. The greater the percentage of raw, living food in your diet, the greater the health benefits.

Raw foods are considered "living" foods because they contain life energy producing enzymes. Enzymes are a long string of amino acids that exists in every living thing that makes normal cellular function possible. They act as a catalyst for chemical reactions in cells, which means that they either initiate or speed up chemical processes. Many chemical processes require high speed to react appropriately, so you could look at enzymes as life supporting engines of cellular chemical reactions!

Enzymes are responsible for initiating the digestion of foods, which is the primary reason that raw foods are so valuable to the body. In essence, raw foods bring their own enzymes to the party, making it easier for our bodies to digest them. This is not the case with cooked foods.

> *Interestingly, for a caterpillar to turn into a butterfly, it digests itself using enzymes triggered by hormones.*

This is where raw, living foods play a very significant role.

Enzymes are very sensitive to heat above 118°F. When food is cooked, steamed, canned, pasteurized, baked, or boiled above 120°F, it loses virtually all of its enzyme activity. So in the process of digestion, the body must borrow enzymes from the body rather than from the food itself, resulting in a drain on our system. This is why you may feel sluggish after eating a cooked meal.

More on Phytochemicals
As previously stated, plants convert solar energy from the sun into complex chemical compounds called *phytochemicals*. Phytochemicals, also called phytonutrients, are naturally occurring plant chemical compounds that can have protective qualities for human health.

Consuming a rainbow of fruits and vegetables every day gives your body a wide range of phytochemical-nutrients that science now knows will protect you from almost every chronic disease known. One of the best ways to be assured of getting enough of these powerhouse phytonutrients, such as flavonoids, bioflavonoids, or carotenoids, is to simply blend and drink it all—seeds, skin (with a few exceptions), and flesh. These nutritional powerhouses exhibit a cornucopia of health-giving benefits.

Red Fruits and Vegetables are known for lycopene, quercetin, and other antioxidants that neutralize free radicals, regulate blood pressure, and reduce the risk of prostate cancer, among other things. Nature's red fruits include strawberries, cranberries, and watermelon. Red vegetables include red peppers, radishes, and beets.

Orange and Yellow Fruits and Vegetables contain beta-carotene, zeaxanthin, potassium, and vitamin C. They are abundant in antioxidants and other phytonutrients that are good for your skin, joints, eyes, and heart and also decrease your risk of cancer. Nature's orange and yellow fruits include oranges, mangoes, and peaches. Orange and yellow vegetables include sweet potatoes, corn, and pumpkin.

Green Fruits and Vegetables contain ample stores of chlorophyll, lutein, folate, and calcium. They neutralize free radicals, strengthen the immune system, regulate blood pressure, and reduce cancer risks. Green fruits include avocados, kiwi, and honeydew melons. Green vegetables include leafy greens, asparagus, and peas.

Blue and Purple Fruits and Vegetables contain lutein, resveratrol, and various flavonoids. Evidence indicates that these purple pigments protect our brains as we age, strengthen our immune system, support healthy digestion, and have anti-carcinogenic properties. Blue and purple fruits include blueberries, plums, and grapes. Blue and purple vegetables include eggplant, cabbage, and endive.

White Fruits and Vegetables contain allicin, an antifungal compound found in the garlic and onion family, along with beta-glucans and lignans, which have powerful immune-boosting properties. These powerful phytochemical-nutrients are also known to balance hormones and reduce the risk of colon, breast, prostate, and hormone-related cancers. Nature's white fruits include bananas, pears and dates. White vegetables include onions, potatoes, honeydew melons, and cauliflower.

This list only shows the properties of *known nutrients* in plants, but cannot give us the "whole" story. The bottom line is to "let food be thy medicine and medicine be thy food" by consuming a diet high in raw, living whole-foods! Always remember, when you're consuming a diet high in raw, living foods, the whole is greater than the sum of the parts.

New Earth Food Principle #2
Consume the Right Type of
Salt, Oil, and Sugar

The second New Earth Food Principle is to consume the right type of salt, oil and sugar! If your body has been sending you an S-O-S signal, it's time to answer the call! It's most likely your body's attempt to warn you that you might be using "the wrong type of salt, oil, and sugar!"

The Wrong and Right Type of Salt
The wrong type of salt is refined salt; a salt that is poison to your body! Refined salt is 97.5 percent sodium chloride and 2.5 percent chemicals such as moisture absorbents, anti-caking agents and possibly an iodine-containing compound. Dried at over 1,200°F, the excessive heat substantially alters the natural molecular structure of the salt, regardless of whether it is land or sea salt. What remains after salts are heat-treated and chemically cleaned is a degraded structure of sodium chloride, a form of salt that your body identifies as something unnatural. This type of salt is inorganic, which means the body doesn't identify it as "real food." Some even refer to refined salt as "white poison!"

When salt has been refined, naturally-occurring trace minerals have been removed, thus the natural structure has been broken down. Afterwards, poisonous forms of iodide and fluorine are generally added.

Iodine and fluorine, in the form provided in table salt, are known to catalyze the production of cancer-causing nitrates in the stomach.

Researchers and physicians around the world have found that a diet high in refined salt contributes to a number of health risks, such as high blood pressure, heart disease, stroke, and certain kinds of cancers. Still, the right kind of salt is as fundamental to our life as air and water, and without it we could not exist.

The right type of salt is a mineral complex with a structure that looks like plant fronds under a microscope. A whole-food sea salt is an unheated, unrefined product that contains all of the natural elements of the pristine seas, concentrated and dried by the sun. When dissolved in water or bodily fluids, this type of salt produces an electrolytic conductivity that allows for the instantaneous flow of energy throughout the watery cellular medium of our bodies. The structure of salt, or the configuration of the mineral electrolytes, is a critical indicator of the life force held within it.

> "Salt is born of the purest of parents: the sun and the sea."
> –Pythagoras (580 BC – 500 BC)

Celtic Sea Salt® is a high-quality, whole-food salt that is in its complete, natural, alkalizing form of raw electrolytes. It is harvested off the coast of France using methods originating with the Celts millennia ago that contains a full spectrum of essential trace minerals. While it is still mostly sourced from France, it is also sourced from coastal areas of Guatemala, Hawaii, Colima (Mexico), Portugal and the Fossil River in Spain. This salt is harvested by hand with the intention of preserving its natural, whole state; a salt you can definitely trust!

When I use salt, you can be sure it's Celtic Sea Salt®!

The Wrong and Right Type of Oil

The wrong type of oil comes from processed vegetable oils, such as seed oils. In recent years, it's become increasingly clear that seed oils are one of the most damaging components of our modern-day diet. When heated, these type of oils contain excessive amounts of oxidized omega-6 linoleic acid, a polyunsaturated fatty acid (PUFA). The biological damage it causes is even worse than that caused by refined salt or high fructose corn syrup.

According to ophthalmologist Dr. Chris Knobbe, who has researched the matter extensively, a preponderance of processed vegetable seed oils in our diet is a major factor in virtually all chronic metabolic and degenerative diseases, including age-related macular degeneration.

The most damaging PUFA oils to avoid are: canola oil, grapeseed oil, corn oil, soybean oil, generic vegetable oil, walnut oil, cottonseed oil, sesame oil, peanut oil, margarine, and yes, even flaxseed oil. These processed seed oils are known to promote inflammation, damage the cells that line your blood vessels and your mitochondria, and lower your antioxidant defenses by stripping your liver of glutathione.

The right type of oil, and the only oil I ever use, is organic, cold-pressed olive oil high in polyphenols (micronutrients that we get through certain plant-based foods), and is the only oil I recommend. I also recommend that we use it sparingly, mostly because oils are not in a whole plant-food form, and that includes olive oil. The good news, however, is that olive oil that is high in polyphenols is packed with antioxidants and loads of potential health benefits. Organic, extra-virgin olive oil from Crete and Morocco appears to contain the highest polyphenol levels. How you can tell if olive oil has polyphenols is to check the label to see if the olives were harvested early. Polyphenols accumulate in the olives earlier than the oil and steadily decreases as the fruit matures.

When I use oil, you can be sure it's Olive Oil high in polyphenols!

The Wrong and Right Type of Sugar

The wrong type of sugar is sugar that has been refined from naturally occurring sugars found in sugar cane. Having all its naturally-occurring, health providing minerals and polyphenols completely removed, refined sugar has been linked to increased risk of obesity, insulin resistance, type-2 diabetes, and heart disease. It has also been linked to a higher likelihood of depression, dementia, liver disease, and certain types of cancer.

The right type of sugar, on the other hand, is natural sugar in its whole-food form. This type of natural sugar is found in everything from fresh fruit, raisins, dates, raw honey, maple syrup, date sugar, raw coconut nectar, agave, raw sugar, and monk fruit… natural sugar that nature designed for us to eat!

Natural, whole-food sugars are combined with and balanced by other naturally-occurring ingredients, such as structured water, vitamins, minerals, salts, and fiber, as well as other beneficial elements, known and unknown. It's the complex, life-giving structure of a whole food versus a refined food that always makes the difference.

Always keep in mind that sugary FRUITS are not your enemy... the enemy is the combination of fruits and fats, especially the wrong type of fats!

New Earth Food Principle #3
Eat Locally Grown, Seasonal Foods

The third New Earth Food Principle is to eat locally and seasonally. Foods grown close to home are saturated with an abundance of phytochemical-nutrition because it is picked close to its ripened peak. Eating locally and seasonally can also be healthy for the environment. Buying foods purchased from your "food shed," loosely defined as farms within 100 miles of your home, helps to curtail the issue with carbon and global warming. Shipping and trucking food from every corner of the world requires millions of gallons of gasoline for transportation, not to mention all of the pollution it releases into the environment, just getting to the supermarket.

Produce purchased from the supermarket has been picked unripened then shipped in cold regeration for days or even weeks, whereas produce purchased from a local farmer's market has often been picked within 24 hours of your purchase. This freshness not only affects the flavor of your food, but the nutritional value as well, which declines with time and changes in temperature.

Spending your money at a local farmer's market not only supports your health and the environment, but it also supports the livelihood of farmers in your community as well as the local economy.

Eat Seasonal Foods

Seasonal eating is a sustainable way of eating that has numerous health advantages. This lifestyle encourages you to only eat fruits and vegetables that are in season for your geographic area, such as eating pears in the fall, oranges in the winter, asparagus in the spring, tomatoes in the summer, and so on.

Seasonal foods are fresher, tastier and more nutritious than food consumed out of season. Even though we all like to eat strawberries or watermelon year-round, the best time to eat them is when they can be purchased directly from a local grower shortly after harvest.

As you know, for those of us who do not live in the tropics, there are four growing and harvesting seasons:

- *Autumn* is the time to eat lots of grapes, apples, persimmons, and other fall fruits, along with seasonal salads, steamed or roasted squashes, and other root vegetables.
- *Winter* is the time to focus on rest, meditation, and storing up energy. Strengthening, warming foods like soups and stews are good to eat (unless you live in the tropics).
- *Spring* is the time when a new cycle begins. A diet of more cleansing and revitalizing foods like asparagus, dandelions, other leafy greens and sprouts harmonize the body in this season of rejuvenation and growth.
- *Summer* is the time when fruits are abundant, so a raw fruit diet low in fat is recommended during this season.

SEASONAL FOOD CHART

Spring (March - May)

avocados	cauliflower	lettuce	greens
bananas	navel oranges	mushrooms	parsnips
cherries	papayas	raspberries	peas
artichokes	pineapples	watercress	herbs
asparagus	celery	potatoes	carrots
shallots	cucumbers	rhubarb	beetroots
grapefruits	garlic	snap beans	radishes
lemons	apples	spinach	kale
mangoes	plums	squash	watercress
broccoli	strawberries	onions	parsley.
cabbage	leeks	dandelion	

Summer (June - August)

apricots	cherries	garlic	onions
blueberries	grapefruits	peppers	potatoes
artichokes	grapes	peaches	spinach
cabbage	honeydew	Persian melons	gooseberries
carrots	celery	strawberries	mangoes
peas	corn	lettuce	squash
boysenberries	cucumbers	mushrooms	tomatoes
cantaloupes	lemons	okra	watercress
zucchini	nectarines	valencia oranges	radishes
cauliflower	eggplant	watermelons	raspberries.

Fall (September - November)

Apples	lemons	escarole	sweet potatoes
cantaloupes	plums	peppers	turnips
dates	chili peppers	peas	spinach
artichokes	cucumbers	kale	cauliflower
broccoli	papayas	kiwis	sweet corn
lettuce	pears	peaches	tomatoes
cranberries	blackberries	raspberries	squash
grapefruits	French beans	parsnips	watercress
grapes	endive	onions	chestnuts
cabbage	leeks	yams	beetroot
carrots	Persian melons	pumpkins	celeriac.
celery	persimmons	lettuce	
honeydews	figs	potatoes	

Winter (December - February)

Grapefruits	cabbage	pears	mushrooms
lemons	persimmons	celery	potatoes
kiwis	tangelos	spinach	tomatoes
navel oranges	Brussels sprouts	squash	parsnips
artichokes	cauliflower	turnips	rutabaga
broccoli	tangerines	lettuce	

This list was compiled from the Third Street Farmer's Market in Santa Monica, California.

New Earth Food Principle #4
Proper Food Combining

The fourth New Earth Food Principle is to properly combine the types of foods you eat. While certain food-combining principles are as ancient as the Mosaic Covenant (the Jewish law requiring the separating of meat and dairy), some of today's top nutritional researchers report that some foods are digested differently, thus should be eaten separately and at different times. There are plenty of books on the subject, and I recommend reading up on this practice, especially if you have issues with digestion.

Fruits and non-starchy vegetables are digested quickly and easily. Other foods require more time and specialized enzymatic functions. The most important rule is to separate a meal of carbohydrate-rich foods such as rice, bananas and carrots from protein-rich foods such as beans, nuts and seeds.

According to the studies of Dr. Herbert M. Shelton, one of the greatest natural hygienists and the father of food combining, there are sound physiological reasons for eating, separately, foods that require different digestive enzymes and gastric juices in the mouth, stomach and small intestines.

- Starchy foods require an alkaline digestive medium, which is supplied initially in the mouth by the enzyme ptyalin.
- Protein foods require an acid medium for digestion, which is supplied in the stomach by acid enzymes and hydrochloric acid.

Hydrochloric acid destroys ptyalin and suspends the digestion of starches. Undigested starch in the stomach interferes with the digestion of protein. It absorbs and neutralizes the enzyme pepsin, which is required for the digestion of protein.

In short, acid and alkaline digestive mediums neutralize each other. Therefore, if you eat a starch food with a protein food, digestion may be impaired or completely arrested. These undigested foods can cause various kinds of digestive disorders.

> Another newly discovered, food-combining rule:
> Never combine fruits with fats!

Most vegans, vegetarians and even raw foodists are consuming way too many fats in their diets in the form of nuts, seeds and oils. The problem arises when a high-fat diet is combined with a high-fruit diet. Ultimately, fruits and fats do not mix! When eaten together, they can create a health-debilitating perfect storm.

Dr. Neal Barnard, in his book, *How to Reverse Diabetes,* scientifically proved that, over time, undigested fats can accumulate around the membrane (skin) of our cells, which inhibits insulin's ability to carry glucose into the cells to be converted into energy and out of the bloodstream. If glucose is allowed to build up in our bloodstream, everything from insulin resistance to type-2 diabetes can occur. Even Candida can grow out of control in its attempt to consume the sugar.

Therefore, the more fat you eat when consuming a high fruit, high carbohydate diet, the less effective insulin is at getting glucose into the cells and out of the bloodstream; this is why, a high fat, high protein diet works, such as Keto and Paleo. No sugar, no problem; you can lose weight because there's not a build-up of glucose in the blood stream! However, when consuming this type of unnatural diet long term, they might just eventually create unnatural side-effects, such as acidosis.

So, how about a more natural alkaline diet, a diet that nature intended for us! High carbohydrates, high fruit but NO fat!

It's as simple as that!

New Earth Food Principle #5
Follow the Circadian Rhythm

The fifth New Earth Food Principle is to follow certain daily cycles known as the circadian rhythm. Circadian refers to the regular recurrence of cycles of activity that occur approximately every 24 hours, or one full day. The rhythm is linked to the sun and the moon's light-dark cycle. While sleep cycles are the most common studied by science, it has also been found that if one's daily eating patterns are in tune with these naturally occurring rhythms, people notice a tremendous increase in their overall health, energy and well-being.

According to natural hygienists, there are three cycles associated with the circadian rhythm: (1) consumption (eating and digesting); (2) assimilation (extracting nutrients and assimilating); and (3) elimination (purging and releasing). Each has its own eight-hour period during which its activities are the most heightened.

The *consumption* cycle is from noon until 8 PM. This is the time when the body is most capable of efficiently taking in and digesting food.

The *assimilation* cycle is from 8 PM until 4 AM. This is the time the body is extracting nutrients and assimilating what it needs.

The *elimination* cycle is from 4 AM until noon. This is the time when the body is gathering wastes and preparing them for elimination.

Step 1: The Consumption Cycle

Food should be eaten between noon and 8 PM. This is when your body is in the consumption cycle. The consumption cycle occurs when the body is predisposed to eating and digesting food, and allotting the energy to do so. Chinese medicine has long taught that our digestive fire increases and decreases according to the position of the sun. Thus, because the sun is at its highest and greatest intensity from noon until 3 PM, these three hours, according to this tradition, are the most optimal time to consume the majority of our food.

Step 2: The Assimilation Cycle

Food should *not* be eaten between 8 PM and 4 AM. This is when your body switches from the consumption cycle to the assimilation cycle and starts the process of extracting and assimilating the nutrients from the food you've eaten during the consumption cycle. Hence, after the food you've consumed has been digested, energy is needed to extract and utilize the nutrients the body requires for optimal function. If food is eaten after 8 PM, your body is forced out of the assimilation cycle and back into the consumption cycle, diverting energy away from proper nutrient extraction and uptake and stressing your digestive system.

Step 3: The Elimination Cycle
Food should *not* be eaten between 4 AM to noon. This is when your body is in the elimination cycle. Food consumed prior to the completion of the elimination cycle not only severely retards the process of eliminating the accumulated wastes from the body, it also throws the rhythm of the three cycles into turmoil. The best way to flush out the accumulated waste during this cycle is to drink 16 to 32 ounces of purified, structured water upon waking. Then, if you feel the need to eat, consume fruit only until noon as fruits require very little digestive energy. They also hold the plant kingdom's honor of being nature's greatest food for cleansing waste from the physical body. But if you can, no calories at all until noon, even from fruits. Then break the fasting elimination cycle around noon... break-fast... with lots of seasonal fruits! Your body will be glad you did!

New Earth Food Principle #6
Feast while you Fast

The sixth New Earth Food Principle is to "feast while you fast." Studying a range of organisms, from yeast and roundworms to rodents and monkeys, intermittent fasting researchers found that their maximum life span could be increased up to 50 percent, simply by underfeeding and intermittently fasting them. Researchers discovered that undereating reduces the incidence of neurological disease, age-related cancer, cardiovascular disease, and immune deficiencies in rodents, while a high-calorie intake or overfeeding increased the risk for all degenerative diseases, such as cardiovascular disease, various types of cancers, type-2 diabetes, and stroke.

Undereating was also shown to have a positive effect on brain function and debilitating diseases such as Alzheimer's, Parkinson's and strokes.

Undereating seems to protect neurons (a cell that transmits nerve impulses) against degeneration and stimulates the production of new neurons from stem cells, which may increase the ability of the brain to resist aging and restore function after an injury. While vitamins, minerals and antioxidants may improve the health of the brain, it was shown that the major factor for brain health is undereating and an increase in the time between meals.

Researchers at the University of California, Berkeley, showed that healthy mice, given only 5 percent fewer calories than mice allowed to eat freely, experienced a significant reduction in *cell proliferation* in several tissues, considered an indicator for cancer risk. However, mice that ate less calories instead of just reducing food intake, lived a longer, healthier life.

Cell proliferation is the increase in cellular division that takes place just before genetic repair is made, and cancer is essentially the uncontrolled division of cells. It was discovered that a cell will try to fix any damage that has occurred to its DNA, but if it divides before it has a chance to fix the damage, then that damage passes on to the offspring cells. Slowing down the rate of cell proliferation essentially buys time for the cells to repair genetic damage. This was, indeed, very significant research!

Substantial calorie reduction (up to 50 percent in some studies), not only reduces the rate of cell proliferation, but it can extend maximum life span from 30 to 70 percent of a variety of organisms, including rats, flies, worms, and yeast. It was found that mice on a 33 percent reduced calorie diet exhibited significantly decreased cell proliferation rates for skin, breast and T (lymphocyte) cells. The greatest effect was seen after one month on the regimen, when proliferation of skin cells registered only 61 percent of that for mice fed freely. The surprising finding came with the results of the more modest 5 percent reduced calorie diet that was fed intermittently. Mice in this group had skin cell division rates that were 81 percent of those for mice fed freely.

So, even just a small reduction in calories makes a big difference in terms of your body's healing power.

Researchers discovered that fasting every other day also decreased the chance of breast cancer. In all cases, division rates for breast cells were reduced the most. Mice with the lowest calorie diet had breast cell proliferation results that were only 11 percent of those in the controlled group; mice fed intermittently had results that were 37 percent of those in the controlled group. Undereating, along with intermittent fasting, was also found to enhance insulin sensitivity and lower risk of heart disease.

The problem?
We're overtaxing our digestive systems by not following nature's circadian rhythms. Our bodies need time to digest, assimilate and eliminate waste. If waste is allowed to accumulate, our "inner seas" become toxic and acidic, which sets up a breeding ground for reducer organisms, such as viruses, bacteria, candida, and fungus to overgrow in their attempt to clean up the toxic mess. Reducer organisms are like roaches that show up in kitchens where there's left over food particles.

In essence, "if ya feed 'em, they're going to come!"

The solution?
Stop feeding them! Eat less and fast often on easily digestible organic fruits and vegetables. These "fast exit foods," along with intermittent fasting, gives your body the time it needs to "clean house!" When your internal environment is "swept free" of toxic wastes, your body will be functioning at peak performance.

But what if I get hungry between meals?

When you begin to "feast while you fast," it's normal to feel a little hungry between meals. Over the years, our bodies have adapted to eating three "square" meals a day. However, if you feel hungry, try feeding your skin with a little sunlight! Melatonin, triggered by darkness, can also trigger the sensation of hunger; and low levels of vitamin D levels, triggered by a lack of sunlight, can also trigger fat storage.

So, if you're overweight and always hungry, simply go outside and expose your skin to the early morning rays of the sun. That means, if you *eat light, you'll become light!*

New Earth Food Principle #7
Eat Your Chosen Fuel Food Plan

The seventh New Earth Food Principle is to choose your individual *fuel food* plan. This means that you'll choose a plan that best fits each transitional pH stage you might be going through. With all three plans, the heart of the transformational message is to make sure you understand how important it is to *burn the right types of foods for fuel into your body's internal environment;* that is, to understand the importance of eating a diet high in phytochemical-nutrient-rich plant foods.

Just as the grade of gasoline we burn in our car's engine affects the outer environment in a positive or negative way, the grade of food we burn in our body's engine (your cell's mitochondria) affects our internal environment in a positive or negative way.

Gasoline fuel is classified by three grades: *regular, midgrade,* and *premium.* Likewise, *fuel food* can be classified by these same three grades:

>*Regular* is classified as Level One
>The beginner fuel food plan
>
>*Midgrade* is classified as Level Two
>The intermediate fuel food plan
>
>*Premium* is classified as Level Three
>The master fuel food plan

As previously stated, when making any type of dietary change, you should always consider taking enough time to transition. In working with thousands of clients over the years, I discovered that if I offered them an "up level" dietary *fuel food* plan, the shift would become more permanent. Obviously, the more a person continues to "level up" their *fuel food* plan until they've reached the top *master fuel food plan,* the greater the rewards.

Instead of following "man's" scientific way of eating that's based on fats, calories, carbohydrates, and protein, the three fuel food plans in this book are designed according to "nature's" way of eating, which is centered on the type of foods that will FUEL your cells with LIGHT ENERGY, as detailed in my *New Earth Diet* book.

So, let's get started!

LEVEL ONE
The Beginner Fuel Food Plan

80% Alkaline Foods—20% Acid Foods
50% Raw—50% Cooked

Level One is regular fuel food—the beginner transformational fuel food plan. It's a transitional fuel food plan for those who have been eating a highly acidic, animal-based, processed-food diet. This plan is centered around a plant-based, organic, whole-foods diet that places emphasis on fruits, vegetables, gluten-free grains, beans, nuts and seeds. On this plan, you'll follow the 80/20 Plan—80% alkaline foods and 20% acid foods—50% raw foods and 50% cooked.

80% Alkaline Foods
Fruits, green leafy vegetables, all vegetables and sea vegetables

20% Acid Foods
Grains, legumes, alcohol, nuts, seeds, and processed organic whole foods

Completely Eliminate

Animal foods, refined salt, refined sugar, PUFA seed oils, wheat, processed junk food

This means that you can include:

- A few processed organic whole foods, i.e., apple cider vinegar and raw coconut aminos.
- All the fruits and vegetables you desire, but never eat fruit with fat.
- A small serving of organic gluten-free brown rice grains, beans, nuts and seeds.
- A small serving of Celtic sea salt, olive oil, and natural sweeteners such as agave or honey.

Your Level One regular fuel food plan would look like this:

- For breakfast, enjoy a large bowl of seasonal fruits or a smoothie.
- For lunch or dinner, enjoy a large plate of leafy green salad, steamed or roasted veggies, and a small portion of beans, brown rice or brown rice pasta.

    Note: Personally, I only eat two meals a day. I generally enjoy a large fruit meal or smoothie around 12 PM, and a large veggie meal around 4 PM.

Imagine looking at your lunch or dinner plate. At least 80% of the foods you see on your plate are foods from the alkaline food list and no more than 20% would be foods from the acidifying food list—50% of your daily plan would be eaten fresh and raw and 50% would be eaten lightly grilled, baked or steamed.

LEVEL ONE
The Beginner Fuel Food Ideas

BREAKFAST IDEAS

Level One is regular fuel food—the beginner fuel food plan. The first meal of the day is a *fruit fuel food plan*. This means that you can enjoy a bowl of seasonal fruits or smoothie. Remember that fruits are cleansers and are acceptable foods to consume during the morning elimination cycle for beginner fasters. So enjoy as much as you want! But never consume fat with fruit!

- Enjoy a fruit smoothie. Blend 2 cups of raw coconut water, or fruit juice, with any fruit in season. One of my simple favorites is to blend fresh pineapple or mango with raw coconut water.

- How about a fruit salad with your favorite tropical fruits in season? Enjoy it plain or drizzle with date sauce (4 Medjool dates, 1 cup water, and blend until creamy). One of my favorite morning yummies is mashed bananas, grated apples and date sauce!

- Try blending 1 banana and several pitted dates with a cup of water for a smoothie delight. If it's wintertime and you want to warm yourself up, try adding a shake of cayenne pepper!

- Enjoy a fruit smoothie with a few leafy greens. Blend a handful of stemmed kale or spinach with your choice of fresh organic fruit, such as mango, pineapple, banana, and/or papaya, and water. The fiber in fruit gives this smoothie a creamy texture.

- Or, if you're like most and don't have a lot of time in the morning, simply add 1 to 2 tablespoons of my *Alkalize Yourself* powder to your smoothie or juice recipe of choice! You'll be *alkalizing* glad you did!

- Or, why not begin your day with one of my favorite juices? Juice 3 apples, 1 unpeeled lemon, a 1" piece of fresh ginger, 2 beets (let's pretend that they're a fruit!); then, if you want to take it up a "hot notch," add ½ habanera pepper. It'll clean the stagnation out of your liver like nothing else!

- Sometimes, I just like to keep it simple: one fruit at a time. Try a bowl of mangoes or papayas, grapes, peaches, pears, or some watermelon, whichever fruit is in season you enjoy the most.

- Or, simply juice 1 whole lemon (peel and all), add it to a quart jar with 2 tablespoons raw Active Manuka honey, fill with water, shake, and drink. This will start your day cleaning out the accumulated acid wastes, for sure!

Note: Make sure to give yourself at least 4 hours between any type of fruit or sugary consumption before eating fats!

LUNCH AND DINNER IDEAS

The main meal of the day is a heavier fuel food plan with lots of vegetables and a small amount of rice, beans, gluten-free brown rice pasta. Enjoy all of the alkalizing vegetables you want!

- My favorite transitional meal includes a small amount of gluten-free organic brown rice pasta tossed with crushed garlic, salt, chopped basil, and lots of cherry tomatoes cut in quarters. Remember, fats and carbs (sugar) don't mix so I never recommend tossing your pasta with olive oil. Serve with a large bed of baby arugula, tossed with your favorite oil-free salad dressing.

- For a delicious Italian taste-bud delight, create a bountiful bowl of organic Roma tomatoes cut in quarters, tossed with Cannellini beans, salt, roasted red peppers, and garlic; all stacked high on a plate of chopped radicchio and fraise leaves, tossed with your favorite oil-free dressing.

- For a Greek delight, create a bowl of Fava beans, thinly sliced red onion, quartered grape tomatoes, salt and tossed with several handfuls of baby arugula.
- Or, how about a Greek salad with sliced cucumbers, green bell peppers, tomatoes, red onion slivers, raw goat feta, a dash of dill, oregano, salt, and olive oil with a large side-serving of roasted veggies?
- If it's wintertime, enjoy a bowl of red beans, cayenne pepper, chopped red onions, and tossed with escarole greens.
- Or, how about a large bowl full of heirloom black rice, grilled asparagus, over a bed of finely chopped radicchio, all tossed with your favorite fat-free salad dressing?
- Enjoy a large leafy green salad tossed with steamed potato cubes, quartered grape tomatoes, pressed garlic, and salt served with a bowl of your favorite potato leek soup.
- How about a large arugula salad tossed with slices of sun-dried tomatoes, chopped raw olives, organic capers, raw goat feta, tossed in olive oil, along with a bowl of roasted red bell pepper soup?
- For an Italian feast, try making a potato salad with fingerling potatoes, sliced red bell peppers, tossed in pressed garlic, and salt. Then, roast this mixture in the oven until potatoes are slightly brown. Let cool, then toss with a handful of baby arugula. Yum!
- If it's cold outside and you want something to warm your bones, how about a bowl of vegetable bean chili with your favorite salad?

It's as easy as that!

LEVEL TWO
The Intermediate Fuel Food Ideas

90% Alkaline Foods—10% Acid Foods
75% Raw—25% Cooked

Level Two is midgrade fuel food—the intermediate fuel food plan. It is a diet for those who are ready to take that next "level up" step, or for those who aren't (or haven't been) consuming animal-based products for a while and are ready to jump right in! This plan consists of a plant-based, organic, whole-foods diet that places emphasis on equal proportions of fruits and vegetables, and a small amount of nuts and seeds. This diet is animal-free, dairy-free, grain-free, and bean-free. On this plan, 90% of your foods will be from the alkaline food list and 10% will be from the acid food list in the form of nuts and seeds—and 75% raw and 25% cooked. Obviously, the more organic raw plant foods you consume, the better!

This means:

- No processed foods (with a few whole food exceptions.)
- No animal meats, including fish.
- No eggs.
- No cow dairy, including no raw goat cheese.
- No grains or beans.
- You can eat all the fruits and vegetables you desire.
- You can eat a small amount of nuts and seeds.

To be more specific, your Level Two daily menu would look like this:

- For breakfast, you'll enjoy lemon water or freshly-prepared smoothies until 12 PM, or simply eat a big bowl of your favorite fruits in season.
- For lunch or dinner, you might enjoy a large leafy green salad, tossed with your favorite oil-free dressing, and topped with steamed or roasted veggies.

Imagine looking at your dinner plate. Simply put, at least 90% of the foods you see on your plate would be lots of mixed greens and veggies from the alkaline food lists and 10% would be acid foods from the acid food list in the form of nuts and seeds only: 75% of your daily plan would be eaten fresh and raw; 25% would be eaten lightly grilled, baked, or steamed. For example, the food on your lunch or dinner plate would consist of a large green leafy salad tossed with your favorite oil-free dressing, a baked russet or sweet potato, and lightly steamed vegetables on the side.

LEVEL TWO
The Intermediate Fuel Food Ideas

BREAKFAST IDEAS

For a more fruitarian fuel food plan, start your day with your favorite seasonal fruits. Go ahead! Eat them, blend them, or juice them. You can use the same breakfast ideas from Level One if you choose or, if you need a few more ideas, try these!

- How about creating your smoothie with 2 to 3 different fruits such as a whole apple, peeled banana, and the flesh of an orange along with 2 to 3 cups of water. Go ahead; blend the whole fruit, seeds and all; seeds are loaded with phytochemical-nutrients.

Add your favorite dehydrated juice powders such as Acai, or my *Alkalize Yourself* powder blend.

- I love berries, and they are loaded with antioxidants, so how about a "berry good" blend? Blend ½ cup of fresh organic raspberries, blueberries, strawberries, and blackberries with 2–3 cups of purified water or coconut water; add a banana and a superfood powder or juice blend. Go ahead; get creative!

- Take yourself to the tropics one morning with a tropical treat smoothie! Blend 1 cup fresh organic pineapple, mango, and papaya with lots of fresh young coconut water. Add a banana, if you wish!

LUNCH AND DINNER IDEAS

This meal is designed to be the heaviest meal of the day. Enjoy all of the vegetables your heart desires! Vegetables are alkalizing and are the majority of foods to consume during the second fuel food cycle of the day. Enjoy as much as you want. Feel free to always add a few raw nuts or sprouted seeds on top!

- How about a living lentil salad? Place a cup of sprouted lentils tossed with pressed garlic, salt, avocado, grape tomatoes, red onion slivers onto your plate and eat your way to garlic heaven. Enjoy lots of steamed or roasted veggies on the side.

- How about a large bowl of your favorite leafy greens, topped with steamed or roasted organic fingerling potatoes tossed with pressed garlic and salt?

- For a simple yet delicious meal in a bowl, create a colorful array of your favorite chopped veggies, steamed fingerling potatoes tossed with a dash of salt, mint, dill, green onions, avocado, tomatoes and your favorite oil-free dressing.

- Try a large bowl of leafy greens topped with your favorite raw and steamed veggies and a drizzle of sweet oil-free honey mustard dressing.

- For a delicious Italian delight, create a bountiful bowl of organic Roma tomatoes cut in quarters, tossed with roasted red peppers, chopped basil, salt, garlic, stacked high on a plate of chopped radicchio and fraise leaves–drizzled with your favorite oil-free dressing.

- For an autumn feast, how about a baked yam drizzled in raw honey, with a large raw veggie chop salad on the side tossed with oil-free honey mustard dressing?

- Or, how about a raw Greek salad with sliced cucumbers, green bell peppers, tomatoes, red onion slivers, a dash of dill, oregano, salt, and a side of roasted veggies?

- If it's springtime, you might enjoy a large asparagus salad featuring lots of steamed or raw asparagus pieces, sliced cherry tomatoes, diced Valencia oranges, chopped shallots, all tossed in your favorite oil-free dressing, or simply tossed in lemon juice and tarragon.

- If it's summertime, enjoy a small bowl of vegetable soup served with a large chopped veggie salad tossed with an oil-free salad dressing.

- How about a large mixed green salad with lots of avocado and tomato, all tossed in your favorite oil-free dressing and a small bowl of cashew cream of broccoli soup?

- If it's springtime, enjoy a large watercress papaya salad with a bowl of your favorite soup.

- Or, simply enjoy a bowl of "energy soup" made with a handful of baby greens, 1 to 2 cups of sunflower sprouts, ½ avocado, 1 whole apple (peel, seeds and all), and raw coconut water.

LEVEL THREE
The Master Fuel Food Ideas

95% Alkaline Foods—5% Acid Foods
100% Raw
Oil-Free

Level Three is premium fuel food—the master fuel food plan. It's a diet for those who are ready to take that final "level up" step. This plan consists of a 100% raw, oil-free, organic, mostly fruit, plant-based diet that places emphasis on fruits and dark leafy greens, with small amounts of sprouted nuts and seeds. It's for those of you who are ready to go for the highest state of health possible. Try it, even if it's just for 90 days, and see what I mean!

On this plan, you'll follow the 95/5 Plan, but this time it looks like this: 95% alkaline foods in the form of fruits and vegetables, and 5% mildly acid foods in the form of nuts and seeds—100% raw.

The main difference between Level Two and Level Three is that you'll be increasing your intake of fruits and vegetables, eliminating starchy vegetables, and eating everything raw.

This means
- No processed foods (with a few whole food exceptions).

- No animal meats.
- No dairy or eggs.
- No grains or beans.
- No potatoes or other starchy vegetables such as winter squashes.
- No oil.
- Eat all the fruits and leafy vegetables you desire.
- Eat small amounts of starch-free veggies.
- Include small amounts of nuts and seeds.

To be more specific, your Level Three daily menu would look like this:

- Drink purified, structured water until noon.
- For brunch, enjoy a quart of freshly-prepared juice or fruit smoothie.
- For lunch, enjoy lots of seasonal fruits; eat as much as you want.
- For dinner, enjoy a large bowl of raw soup with a leafy green vegetable salad.

Imagine looking at your dinner plate. Simply put, the foods you see on your plate would be leafy greens, and/or vegetables, all tossed with an oil-free salad dressing—100% of your daily food plan would be eaten fresh and raw.

And no! You don't have to spend hours in the kitchen prepping, dehydrating, and preparing fancy raw-food meals; that is, unless you want to. All you have to do is pick, peel and eat—just as if you were living out in the tropics. Or, if you want some raw food chips with your raw soup, try Brad's Raw Chips that are already premade for you and found at most health food stores!

Simply keep in mind that the reason you eat is to fuel the trillions of cells that swim throughout the "inner seas" of your body with foods that supply them with lots of energizing fuel. Fruits, greens and vegetables, along with a small amount of nuts and seeds are the premium fuel foods!

To show you how really simple it is, here's a sample week of menu ideas:

LEVEL THREE
The Master Fuel Food Ideas

BRUNCH (12 PM)

Seasonal fruits are the main fuel for your first meal of the day. It's the time of the day your body needs to not only eliminate any toxic, accumulated waste, but it's also the time every cell in your body requires the extra high-octane energy that only fruits can give.

- Enjoy as much freshly prepared juice as you want.
- If it's summertime, eat as much watermelon as you want.
- Have one of my favorites…a banana date smoothie. Blend 2 bananas with 3 Medjool dates in 16 ounces of water. Simply delicious!
- What about a tropical delight? Blend 1 large mango, 1 banana, 1 small papaya with 1-2 cups of raw coconut water.
- How about a "berry good" smoothie? Blend 1 banana, 1 cup blueberries, 1 cup strawberries, 1 cup raspberries with the juice of 3 oranges?
- Try what I call a mango mania smoothie. Blend 3 mangoes, 1 banana, with 16 ounces of coconut water, and enjoy.

- At least once a week, I enjoy a very simple pineapple coconut smoothie for brunch. I simply blend 1-quart pineapple pieces with 20-ounces raw coconut water. Absolutely off-the-chart delicious!
- Or, how about a simple blend of freshly-prepared orange juice with lots of strawberries? It's one of my favorites.

LUNCH and DINNER IDEAS

Whether you're eating in or out, leafy green salads and raw soups are the high-octane fuel for lunch and/or dinner. Use your imagination, choose your favorite veggies in season, and create your own.

- Enjoy a large zucchini linguini salad! That's right, "raw zucchini pasta," and it's really simple to make. Using a paring knife, shave long strips of organic raw zucchini, or simply use a Spirooli Spiral Slicer (you can find it online). Simply place your zucchini pasta in a bowl and toss it with pressed garlic, freshly chopped basil, and lots of cherry tomatoes sliced in half, all tossed with some oil-free pesto, and served on a bed of arugula.
- If you're having lunch or dinner out, have a large Romaine lettuce salad with tomatoes and avocado tossed in an oil-free dressing. (I usually carry my own dressing everywhere I go…just in case!)
- How about being creative and making a bowl of raw soup and salad meal from the ingredients that you love the most?
- Summertime? How about a mono fruit meal for lunch? Eat as many bananas, or mangoes, or peaches you want! Or, have your favorite smoothie!
- Enjoy a bowl of gazpacho soup served with a small, chopped veggie salad, tossed in your favorite oil-free dressing.

- How about a great Greek salad tonight with a bowl of raw cucumber dill soup?

- If it's springtime, how about having a delicious salad bowl of your favorite greens tossed in your favorite oil-free dressing, served with a bowl of raw tomato basil soup?

- Or, how about a salsa lettuce wrap with a bowl of gazpacho avocado soup?

These are but menu ideas for you to tap into your own creative chef who desires to be born! But for those of you who just don't have the time and would like to tap in to my personal creative chef, most of these recipe ideas can be found the recipe section of my book, *The New Earth Diet*. Bon appétit!

Fast With Every New Moon

Because you've said YES to *The New Earth Fast*, you're most likely discovering, as I did, that following nature's ebb and flow is not only the key to a healthy immune system and a long and prosperous life, it is also the key to help you prepare your physical body for the shift of the ages.

The *ebb* is the outgoing, releasing or "letting go of" phase—when the water draws itself from the shore. The *flow* is the incoming, receiving or "taking hold of" phase—when water rises and returns to the shore again in response to the gravitational pull of the moon. You can also view it as the sea's out breath and in breath!

Now that you have experienced what it feels like to fast, forgive, and pray during the 7-day new moon phase, you now know its transformational power, and will most likely be excited about your next *New Earth Fast*. I know I AM!

Before every new moon fast, be sure to check your saliva pH to determine which level you're ready for; hopefully you're ready to "level up!" In some cases, there can be pockets of acidity in the body that may take time to eliminate, so don't be discouraged if your saliva pH is still in beginner range. Just "stay the course" until your physical body is ready to shed its skin in preparation for the shift from physical consciousness into spiritual consciousness.

Every time you fast during the 7-day new moon phase, a momentum is building, so keep the faith! After your first few monthly new moon fasts, your body will have become so in tune with nature and nature's cycles of change that you'll instinctively arrange your life around these seven very powerful transformational days.

The time has come.
The time to SHIFT is now.
The New Earth Fast is how!

If you would like to have the support of others who are fasting every month during the 7-day new moon phase, please go to my website @ tonitoney.com and become a member of our *New Earth Times Club.*

For those of you who are ready to go the extra mile and reach the highest level of mastery, join our SHIFT NOW Master Course @ tonitoney.com

REFERENCE NOTES

1 – The Great Awakening

Toni's Prophetic Awakenings—reference, the Angelic Presence of God who speaks within her.

Origin of the Greek word, Apocalypse: https://www.dictionary.com/browse/apocalypse

Seven Churches of Revelation in Turkey: https://en.wikipedia.org/wiki/Seven_churches_of_Asia#:~:text=According%20to%20Revelation%201%3A11,churches%20in%20this%20context%20refers

2 – Shift with the New Moon

Dr. Bruce Parker, former chief scientist of NOAA, tides, and the parting of the Red Sea: https://www.dailymail.co.uk/sciencetech/article-2868352/How-Red-Sea-really-parted-Moses-used-knowledge-tides-ensure-safe-crossing-Israelites-instead-waiting-miracle-expert-claims.html

Moses, Pharaoh, Egypt, Israelites, Plagues, Red Sea, Wilderness, Promised Land: https://www.nationalgeographic.com/culture/people-in-the-bible/moses-plagues-miracles-prophet/

Gandhi - https://www.goodreads.com/quotes/760902-we-but-mirror-the-world-all-the-tendencies-present-in

Red Sea and origin of Kosher law: https://www.biblicalarchaeology.org/daily/ancient-cultures/daily-life-and-practice/making-sense-of-kosher-laws/

3 – The Power of New Moon Fasting

Moon Cycles: https://moon.nasa.gov/moon-in-motion/moon-phases/

Moon phases and how they happen: https://spaceplace.nasa.gov/moon- phases/en/

The gravitational pull of the moon and what causes it: https://oceanservice. noaa.gov/education/tutorial_tides/tides02_cause.html

Blood vessels of our planet: https://www.dailymail.co.uk/ sciencetech/article-2141291/The-stunning-blood-vessels-planet- How-river-deltas-change-world--lives-500million-people-reside- shores.html

The testimonies of the Earth's veins: https://www.wearewater.org/en/rivers-the-testimony-of-the-earth-s-veins_352094

Difference between blood and lymph: https://www.vedantu.com/biology/difference-between-blood-and-lymph, Blood and Lymph: https://socratic.org/questions/what-is-the-relationship-between-lymph-and-blood

Main function of our cardiovascular system: https://my.clevelandclinic.org/health/body/21833-cardiovascular-system

Main function of our lymphatic system: https://my.clevelandclinic.org/health/articles/21199-lymphatic-system

The Great Cardiovascular System: https://www.medicalnewstoday.com/articles/cardiovascular-system

The Great Lymphatic System: https://www.medicalnewstoday.com/articles/303087, https://martinswellness.com/blog/post/lymphatic-system

The Lymphatic-Immune System: Inho Choi, Sunju Lee, Young-Kwon Hong, "The New Era of the Lymphatic System: No Longer Secondary to the Blood Vascular System," Cold Spring Harbor Perspectives in Medicine 2, no. 4 (April 2012): a006445, www.ncbi.nlm.nih.gov/pmc/articles/PMC3312397/

Lymphatic System: https://www.livescience.com/26983-lymphatic-system.html

https://www.ncbi.nlm.nih.gov/books/NBK279395/

Professor Arnold Ehret: Mucusless Diet Healing System; 1922; repr., Dobbs Ferry, NY: Ehret Literature Publishing Co, 1994). Lesson 1, Page 19

https://www.ncbi.nlm.nih.gov/pmc/articles/PMC7819965/#:~:text=The%20bacterium%20Chlamydia%20pneumoniae%2C%20which,C.

Robert Morse, ND, The Detox Miracle Sourcebook (Prescott, AZ: Hohm Press, 2004), pp 8–11. Dr. Morse operates a natural health clinic in Florida, specializing in brain and nerve regeneration. See his website at http://www. drmorsesherbalhealthclub.com/

Backed up lymphatic system: Carly Fraser, "Toxins Stored in Your Fat Cells Make You Fatigued and Swollen," LiveLoveFruit, November 8, 2017, https://livelovefruit.com/toxins- stored-in-fat- cells-and-how-to-detox/

Lymphatic vessels recently found in the human brain: https://www.fiercebiotech.com/research/brain-s-recently-discovered-lymphatic-system-linked-to-aging-and-alzheimer-s

Lymphatic Vessels in the brain: https://www.nih.gov/news-events/ nih-research-matters/lymphatic-vessels-discovered-central-nervous- system

Structural and functional features of central nervous system lymphatic vessels. Louveau A, Smirnov I, Keyes TJ, Eccles JD, Rouhani SJ, Peske JD, Derecki NC, Castle D, Mandell JW, Lee KS, Harris TH, Kipnis J. Nature. 2015 Jun 1. doi: 10.1038/nature14432. [Epub ahead of print]. PMID: 26030524.

https://www.nih.gov/news-events/nih-research-matters/brain-cleaning-system-uses-lymphatic-vessels

Internal Acid Rain-buffering systems: https://www.uwa.edu.au/study/-/media/Faculties/Science/Docs/Buffering-systems-in-the-human-body.pdf

Acid Rain and Ecosystems: https://www.smithsonianmag.com/science-nature/acid-rain-and-our-ecosystem-20824120/

Brain on fire: https://healthcare.utah.edu/press-releases/2022/03/nationwide-study-led-u-of-u-health-tests-new-treatment-brain-fire-disease

"Brain Cleaning System Uses Lymphatic Vessels," NIH, Oct 17, 2017, https://www.nih.gov/news-events/nih-research-matters/brain-cleaning- system-uses-lymphatic-vessels.

http://sitn.hms.harvard.edu/flash/2016/how-a-newly-discovered-body-part-changes-our-understanding-of-the-brain-and-the-immune-system/

Germs vs Terrain: https://www.nutritionist-resource.org.uk/memberarticles/germ-theory-vs-terrain-theory-in-relation-to-the-coronavirus

https://www.popsci.com/health/germ-theory-terrain-theory/

4 – The Art of Fasting, Forgiveness and Prayer

The Ancient Art of Fasting: Moses fasted for 40 days and 40 nights: https://biblehub.com/ exodus/34-28.htm

Daniel's Fast: https://en.wikipedia.org/wiki/Daniel_Fast

Intermittent Fasting: Intermittent Fasting: Hutchison, A. T. and Heilbronn, L. K. (2016) Metabolic impacts of altering meal frequency and timing – Does when we eat matter? Biochimie. 124,187-197

Dr. Herbert Shelton: https://www.goodreads.com/author/quotes/4617.Herbert_M_Shelton

Dr. Herbert Shelton: https://www.healthscience.org/shop/fasting-renewal-life-0

"Fill up on Phytochemicals," Harvard Medical School, Feb 1, 2019, https://www.health.harvard.edu/staying-healthy/fill-up-on-phytochemicals

Phytochemicals, https://workwelldaily.com/are-you-eating-yourself-to-death-release-from-phytochemical/

Health benefits of fruit: https://food.unl.edu/NEP/NEP%20Documents/Fruit%20Group.pdf

Health benefits of smoothies: https://www.foodandnutritionjournal.org/volume6number2/smoothies-exploring-the-attitudes-beliefs- and-behaviours-of-consumers-and-non-consumers/

Health benefits of juicing: https://www.ncbi.nlm.nih.gov/pmc/articles/ PMC5438379/

Debbie Krivitsky, https://www.health.harvard.edu/staying-healthy/fill-up-on-phytochemicals

The Electric Universe Theory - https://www.universeofparticles.com/the-electric-universe/

"AICR's New American Plate: A Plant-Based Diet," American Institute for Cancer Research, last updated on April 14, 2021, https://www.aicr.org/cancer-prevention/food-facts/aicrs-new-american-plate/

American Cancer Society. American Cancer Society Dietary Guidelines Advisory Committee Guidelines on diet, nutrition and cancer prevention: reducing the risk of cancer with healthy food choices and physical activity. American Cancer Society; 1996.

Elizabeth Craik, 'Hippocrates and Early Greek Medicine,' in The Oxford Handbook of Science and Medicine in the Classical World, edited by Paul T. Keyser with John Scarborough (New York:

Oxford University Press, 2018), Chapter B4, pp 215–232.

Michael Hickner, https://www.livescience.com/62570-potato-battery-conduct-electricity.html

"Fasting and Mitochondrial Health," The Institute for Functional Medicine, accessed September 20, 2021, https://www.ifm.org/news-insights/fasting-mitochondrial-health/.

Sarah C.P. Williams, "Cells' Mitochondria Work much like Tesla Battery Packs, Study Finds," UCLA, October 14, 2019, https://newsroom.ucla.edu/releases/cells-mitochondria-tesla-battery-packs.

https://novoslabs.com/causes-of-aging-mitochondrial dysfunction/?

Dr. Rai Casey, Rapid Healing and Radical Life Extension (August Dunning, 2020). Spiritual Cleansing: Dr. Rai Casey, https://www.allaboutfasting.com/ fasting-weekends.html

Rai Casey: https://steinerhealth.org/the-benefits-of-fasting/

Alex Carrell - Fossel, Michael B. (2 June 2004). Cells, Aging, and Human Disease. Oxford University Press. p. 504. ISBN 978-0-19-514035-4. page 24.

Carrel, Alexis (1 May 1912). "On the Permanent Life of Tissues Outside of the Organism". Journal of Experimental Medicine. 15 (5): 516–528. doi:10.1084/jem.15.5.516. PMC 2124948. PMID 19867545.

The Ancient Art of Forgiveness: Joe Vitale, http://www.joevitalecertified. com Max Planck: https://en.wikiquote.org/wiki/Max_Planck

Max Planck: https://www.goodreads.com/quotes/1246159-when-you- change-the-way-you-look-at-things-the

Albert Einstein: https://www.quotes.net/quote/42857

Morrnah Nalamaku Simeona, a Hawaiian Kahuna Lapa'au—https://www.beliefnet.com/columnists/ healingandtransformation/2015/03/hooponopono-prayer.html

5 – The New Moon Fast

Saliva pH Testing: https://www.healthline.com/health/ph-of-saliva

pH definition: https://www.merriam-webster.com/dictionary/pH

Norman Walker: https://en.wikipedia.org/wiki/ Norman_W._Walker Fresh Vegetable & Fruit Juices: https://www. amazon. com/

Fresh-Vegetable-Fruit-Juices-Walker/dp/089019033X

Power Boosters: Richard Whelan, 'Lobelia,' accessed 1–25–2019, https://www.rjwhelan. co.nz/herbs%20A-Z/lobelia.html.

Cayenne and Lobelia: Dr. Christopher: 'Cayenne,' 100 Herb Syllabus, The School of Natural Healing, Dr. Christopher's Herbal Legacy, 2004, http://www.herballegacy.com/Cayenne_Herb.html.

"Cayenne," 100 Herb Syllabus, The School of Natural Healing, Dr. Christopher's Herbal Legacy, 2004, https://www.herballegacy.com/Cayenne_Herb.html.

Lobelia: https://www.gaiaherbs.com/blogs/herbs/lobelia Microbiome studies: https://microbiome.ferring.com/

Alkalize Yourself: Organic Sodium: Research shows: M T Morter, Jr., Correlative Urinalysis: The Body Knows Best (Rogers, AR: B.E.S.T. Research Inc., 1987). I have often relied on the superlative wisdom and clarity of Dr. Morter with regards to pH and the acid/alkaline balance.

Organic sodium: M.T. Morter, Jr., Correlative Urinalysis: The Body Knows Best (Rogers, AR: B.E.S.T. Research Inc., 1987). Page 28.

Professional recommendation of Celtic Sea Salt®: https://www.celticseasalt.com/blog/professional-recommendations-for-celtic-sea-salt

Dr. Pavvo Airola: https://www.doctorsbeyondmedicine.com/listing/dry-brushing

Dry Skin Brushing: https://provinceapothecary.com/blogs/news/the-history-of-dry-brushing

Salt scrub benefits: https://sfintercare.com/blog/5-benefits-of-salt-scrub- may-not-know

Take a saltwater bath: Barbara Hendel, MD and Peter Ferreira, Water and Salt: The Essence of Life (German edition 2001; United States: Natural Resources, Inc., 2003).

Cleansing with sea salt baths: https://www.healthline.com/health/ sea-salt-bath

Infrared saunas: www.tonitoney.com

Structured water: https://springaqua. com

Lawrence Armstrong, https://www.hydrationforhealth.com/en/about-us/scientific-committee/list-of-experts/article-prof-lawrence-e-armstrong/

https://education.uconn.edu/2011/02/03/lawrence-armstrong-groundbreaking-research-dehydration/#

Gina Bria, "The Story Behind the Book Quench," Hydration Foundation, https://hydrationfoundation.org/the-story-behind-the-book-quench-by-co-author-gina-bria-2/.

"Interview with Gina Bria on Structured Water," Grow Food Nation, https://growfoodfilm.com/wp-content/uploads/2021/06/ Gina-Bria-Colin Poitras, "Even Mild Hydration Can Alter Our Moods," University of Connecticut, March 27, 2012, https://education.uconn. edu/2012/03/27/even-mild-dehydration-can-alter-our-moods/#.

Pythagoras quote: https:// https://quotepark.com/quotes/739941-pythagoras-salt-is-born-of-the-purest-parents-the-sun-and-th/

Bounce on a rebounder: Albert E Carter, The New Miracles of Rebound Exercise (Nature Distributors, 1988).

NASA studied its benefits: 'Health Benefits of Rebounding,' Wellness Mama, accessed 1-27-2019, https://wellnessmama.com/13915/rebounding-benefits/

Breathe clean air: https://www.vollara.com/ecotarian

Breathe clean indoor air: https://www.vollara.com/ecotarian

Sunlight according to Zane Kime: Zane R Kime, Sunlight (World Health Publications, 1980).

6 – What to Eat After the Fast

Caterpillars shed their skin: https://www.scientificamerican.com/article/caterpillar-butterfly-metamorphosis-explainer/

Carolus Linnaeus quote: https://todayinsci.com/L/Linnaeus_Carolus/ LinnaeusCarolus-Quotations.htm

Dr. Campbell and The China Study quote: https://www.goodreads.com/work/quotes/544922-the-china-study-the-most- comprehensive-study-of-nutrition-ever-conducte

Amount of Protein in Fruits and Vegetables: Data from USDA National Nutrient Database for Standard Reference, Release 25, and Dr. Decuypere's Nutrient ChartsTM

Victoria Boutenko, Green for Life (Ashland, OR: Raw Family Pub, 2005), p. 11.

Katherine Milton, "Diet and Primate Evolution," Scientific American, Aug 1993: 86–93, http://nature.berkeley.edu/ miltonlab/ pdfs/diet_primate_evolution.pdf

Dr. Kathrine Milton quote: (Nutrition Vol.15, No.6, 1999) Dr. Kathrine Milton: http://beforewords.net/

Transformational Food Principle #1 – Consume Plant Foods: Photosynthesis: https://www.livescience.com/51720- photosynthesis.html

Eat a plant-based diet: http://morterbestsessions.com/ph-acidalkaline- balance/

Organic vs. Conventional Growing: Relaena, "Is Organic Always GMO Free?" GMO Awareness, May 5, 2011, http:// gmo- awareness.com/2011/05/05/is- organic-always-gmo-free/

Michael Pollan, interview by Amy Goodman, Democracy Now, Oct 24, 2012. For a transcript see http:// www.democracynow.org/2012/10/24/michael_pollan_ californias_prop_37_fight

Eat Organically Grown Foods: https://www.who.int/news-room/ q-a-detail/pesticide-residues-in-food

Genetically engineered plant materials: Philip Bethge, 'Monsanto Faces Blowback over Cancer Cover-up,' originally appeared in German in Der Spiegel, Issue 43, October 21, 2017, http://www.spiegel.de/ international/world/monsanto-papers-reveal-company-covered-up- cancer-concerns-a-1174233.html.

Walter Danzer, The Invisible Power Within Foods: A Comparison of Organic and Nonorganic (UK ed: Bewusstes Dasiein, AW Danzer, 2016).

Raw Living Foods and Enzymes: https://realrawfood.com/sites/default/files/article/Effects%20of%20Cooking%2C%20by%20.Herbert%20Shelton.pdf

More on Phytochemicals, Rainbow: https://www.health.harvard.edu/blog/phytonutrients-paint-your-plate-with-the-colors-of-the-rainbow-2019042516501

Transformational Food Principle #2 – Eat the right types of salt, oil and sugar: The wrong and right types of salt: https://www.washingtonpost.com/ news/ voraciously/wp/2020/01/06/how-to-choose-the-right-type-of- salt-for- your-recipe

Elizabeth Walling, "Unrefined Sea Salt vs. Table Salt," Aug 23, 2011, http://www. celticseasaltblog.com/unrefined-sea-salt-vs- table-salt-by-elizabeth-walling/

"Iodized Salt," Salt Institute, http://www.saltinstitute.org/ Issues-in-focus/Food- salt-health/Iodized-salt-other-additives

Selina Naturally: "The Missing Ingredients in the Salt Debate," Febr 1, 2011, http://www. celticseasaltblog.com/the-missing- ingredients-in-the- salt-debate/

Barbara Hendel and Peter Ferreira, *Water and Salt: The Essence of Life: The Healing Power of Nature* (Natural Resources, 2003).

The wrong and right types of oil: The case against vegetable oils, https:// mimicnews.com/the-case-against-processed-vegetable-oils, https://www. oliveoiltimes.com/topic/polyphenols https://www. ncbi. nlm.nih.gov/pmc/articles/PMC5877547/

Caldwell B Esselstyn, *Prevent and Reverse Heart Disease: The Revolutionary, Scientifically Proven Nutrition-Based Cure* (New York: Avery, 2007).

Ray Peat, "Unsaturated Vegetable Oils: Toxic," 2006, http:// raypeat. com/articles/ articles/unsaturated-oils.shtml. I drew heavily on this article, in which a great deal of information is brought together and summarized.

T. Colin Campbell, PhD, with Thomas M Campbell II, *The China Study*, pp 69-90. Paavo O Airola, *Are You Confused?* (Phoenix, AZ: Health Plus, 1971), p 96.

Victoria Boutenko, "Green for Life Second Edition," Raw Family, http://www. rawfamily.com/newsletters/green-for- life-2nd-edition

Victoria Boutenko, Elaina Love, and Chad Sarno, *Raw and Beyond: How Omega-3 Nutrition Is Transforming the Raw Food Paradigm* (Berkeley, CA: North Atlantic Books, 2012).

Brian Peskin, "Parent Essential Oils (PEOs): The Difference," http:// www. brianpeskin.com/PEOs.pdf

"Harvard Review of Evidence Verifies That Eating Trans Fats Increases Risk of Heart Disease," Harvard School of Public Health press release, June 23, 1999, www.hsph. harvard.edu/news/press-releases/archives/1999-releasespress06231999.html.

Fiona Haynes, "Do All Foods Listing Hydrogenated Oils Contain Trans Fats?" http://lowfatcooking.about.com/od/faqs/f/hydrogenated.htm

Paul Jaminet, "Pork: Did Leviticus 11:7 Have It Right?"

Stephan Guyenet, PhD, "Does Dietary Saturated Fat Increase Blood Cholesterol? An Informal Review of Observational Studies,"

Whole Health Source, Jan 13, 2011, http:// wholehealthsource. blogspot. com/2011/01/does-dietary- saturated-fat- increase.html

Monica Eng, "Has Your Food Gone Rancid? Consumers May Have Kitchen Full of Dangerous Products and Not Know It,"

Chicago Tribune, March 7, 2012, http:// articles.chicagotribune. com/2012-03-07/features/sc-food-0302- rancidity-20120307_1_ trans-fats-polyunsaturated-oils-food- chain

The wrong and right types of sugar: https://www.healthyeating. org/nutrition-topics/ general/food-groups/fruits - https:// www.healthline. com/health/food-nutrition/monk-fruit-health- benefits#health-benefits

Robert H Lustig, Fat Chance: Beat the Odds Against Sugar, Processed Food, Obesity, and Disease (Penguin Group, 2013).

Mehmet Oz, expert answer to "How Much Sugar Does the Average Person Consume Every Year?" http:// www.sharecare.com/question/sugar-consume-every-year

Bill Sanda, "Double Dangers of High Fructose Corn Syrup," Wise Traditions in Food, Farming and the Healing Arts, Weston Price Foundation, Winter 2003.

Renee Dufault, Blaise LeBlanc, Roseanne Schnoll, Charles Cornett, Laura Schweitzer, David Wallinga,

Jane Hightower, Lyn Patrick, and Walter J Lukiw, "Mercury from Chlor-Alkali Plants: Measured Concentrations in Food Product Sugar," Environmental Health 8, no 2 (2009), doi: 10.1186/1476-069X-8-2

Gabriel Cousins, M.D., MD(H), "My 22 Most Recommended Food Energies," http://www.cultureoflifestore.com/p3/Gabriel+Recommends/pages.html

Bryan Marcel, "Truvia and PureVia Are not Stevia," April 24, 2010, http://www. bryanmarcel.com/truvia-and-purevia-are- not-stevia

Transformational Food Principle #3 – Eat Locally and Seasonally: https:// onlinemph.unc.edu/eating-on-a- budget

Health benefits of eating locally and seasonally: https://www.restorativehealth.org/blog/why-eat-local-and-seasonal-food

Seasonal Food Chart: Compiled from the Third Street Farmer's Market in Santa Monica, California.

Transformational Food Principle #4 - Food Combining: Herbert M Shelton, Food Combining Made Easy (San Antonio: Willow Pub, 1982). Natural Hygiene was a medical movement that flowered in the 1800s.

Herbert Shelton (1895–1984) almost single-handedly revived Natural Hygiene and wrote many books on diet and natural healing. For the many resources of the Natural Hygiene Society, see http://naturalhygienesociety.org/

The Principles of Digestive Physiology Which Decree Correct Food Combining (various articles), The Science of Raw Food, http://www.rawfoodexplained.com/digestive-physiology-and-food-combining/index.html

Dr. Neal Barnard: https://www.pcrm.org/health-topics/diabetes

Transformational Food Principle #5 - Follow Nature's Circadian Rhythms: https://www.nigms.nih.gov/education/fact-sheets/Pages/circadian-rhythms.aspx

Circadian Rhythms: http://blissreturned.wordpress.com/2012/01/17/your-three- natural-body-cycles- this-is-known-as-the-circadian-rhythms/https://chopra.com/articles/circadian-rhythms-and-your-internal-clock- 4-ways-to-sync-with-the-winter-season

Transformational Food Principle #6 – Practice Intermittent Fasting: Michael Mosley and Mimi Spencer, The Fast Diet: Lose Weight,

Stay Healthy and Live Longer with the Simple Secret of Intermittent Fasting, rev. ed. (New York: Atria Books, 2013), p 2.

Sutton, E. F., Beyl, R., Early, K. S., Cefalu, W. T., Ravussin, E. and Peterson, C. M. (2018) Early Time-Restricted Feeding Improves Insulin Sensitivity, Blood Pressure, and Oxidative Stress Even without Weight Loss in Men with Prediabetes. Cell metabolism. 27, 1212-1221 e1213

ABOUT THE AUTHOR

Toni Toney earned her "master's degree" from the highest possible school of learning: NATURE! After almost dying, she discovered that the foods she had been eating had created what we call dis-ease.

The *New Earth Fast* is the program that Toni subscribed to when medicine failed to help her. Her purpose in writing this book is that it might help you, too. After traveling the world for answers, Toni came to understand the power of fasting in healing the body, mind, and emotions, especially during the 7-day New Moon phase.

As the creator of the *New Earth Times* message, she is inviting you to join her in a movement whose time has come—the quest to prepare our physical bodies for the shift of the ages as we infuse our cellular structure with lots of LIGHT.

Welcome to one of the most life-changing, revolutionary way of fasting. along with a transformational way of eating, that produces LIGHT.

So, go ahead—ENLIGHTEN YOURSELF—so your physical body's seven seals can open!

With Love,
Toni Toney

tonitoney.com